D0213093

CASE STUDIES IN
CULTURAL ANTHROPOLOGY

GENERAL EDITORS

George and Louise Spindler

STANFORD UNIVERSITY

MEXICAN-AMERICANS OF SOUTH TEXAS

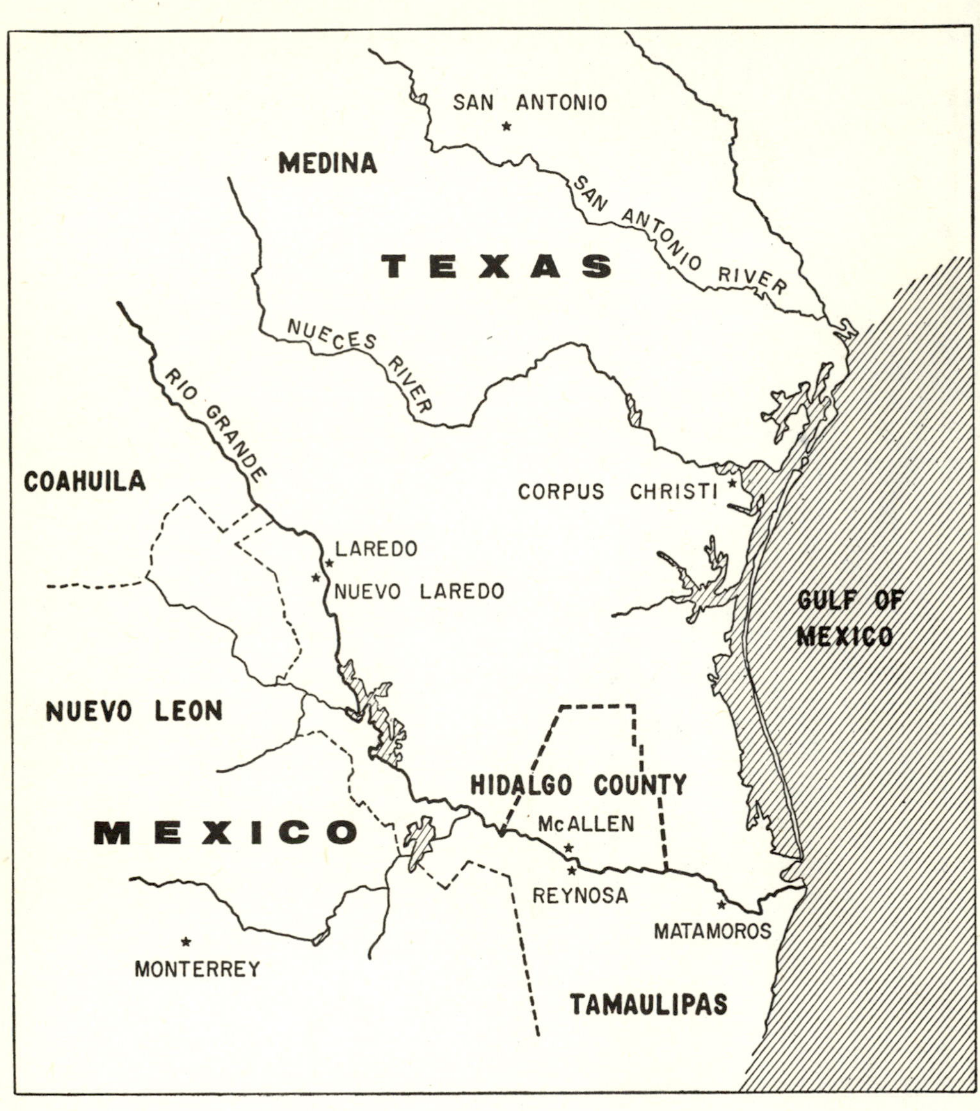
SAN ANTONIO
MEDINA
SAN ANTONIO RIVER
TEXAS
NUECES RIVER
RIO GRANDE
COAHUILA
CORPUS CHRISTI
LAREDO
NUEVO LAREDO
GULF OF MEXICO
NUEVO LEON
HIDALGO COUNTY
McALLEN
MEXICO
REYNOSA
MATAMOROS
MONTERREY
TAMAULIPAS

MEXICAN-AMERICANS OF SOUTH TEXAS

Second Edition

By

WILLIAM MADSEN
University of California,
Santa Barbara

Epilogue by Andre Guerrero

HOLT, RINEHART AND WINSTON, INC.
NEW YORK CHICAGO SAN FRANCISCO ATLANTA
DALLAS MONTREAL TORONTO LONDON SYDNEY

Library of Congress Catalog Card Number: 73-2824
ISBN: 0-03-008431-8
Printed in the United States of America
3456 059 987654321

To the people of La Raza

May their God-given

destiny be fulfilled.

Foreword

About the Series

These case studies in cultural anthropology are designed to bring to students, in beginning and intermediate courses in the social sciences, insights into the richness and complexity of human life as it is lived in different ways and in different places. They are written by men and women who have lived in the societies they write about, and who are professionally trained as observers and interpreters of human behavior. The authors are also teachers, and in writing their books they have kept the students who will read them foremost in their minds. It is our belief that when an understanding of ways of life very different from one's own is gained, abstractions and generalizations about social structure, cultural values, subsistence techniques, and the other universal categories of human social behavior become meaningful.

About the Author

William Madsen was born a United States National in Shanghai, China. He went to school in Manila, and then to Harvard University, Cambridge University in England, and finally to Stanford for his B.A. He did graduate work at the Escuela Nacional de Antropologia, Mexico, and finished his Ph.D. at the University of California, Berkeley. He served with the American Field Service in the British Eighth Army, North Africa, in 1941–1943, and has taught at the University of Texas, the University of California at Berkeley, and at Santa Barbara. In 1963–1964 he was a research associate at the Institute for the Study of Human Problems at Stanford, and is now Professor of Anthropology at University of California, Santa Barbara. He was also acting director of the Institute of Latin American Studies at the University of Texas, and president of the Board of Directors, Centro de Investigaciones Sociales, A.C., Monterrey, Mexico, and was the founder and first president of this organization. He is a fellow of the American Anthropological Association, and is a member of several other scientific societies, including the Sociedad Mexicana de Antropologia. He is author of numerous books concerned with Mexican and Mexican-American cultures, including *Christo-Paganism, A Study of Mexican Religious Syncretism, The Virgin's Children: Life in an Aztec Village Today*, and *Society and Health in the Lower Rio Grande Valley.*

About the Book

This case study provides meaningful detail on aspects of behavior and belief that make the Mexican-American (or Chicano) way of life in South

Texas distinctive—and that give members of *La Raza* satisfactions that are not grasped by most Anglo observers. These very satisfactions and the life-way that makes them possible inevitably come into conflict with Anglo-American culture. The book shows how a member of *La Raza* finds it difficult to become anglicized without losing his friends and his self-respect, given the denial of the validity of cultural pluralism that has been a feature of Anglo-American culture. It also shows how well-meaning people—teachers, public officials, medical personnel, even social workers—frequently misunderstand Mexican-Americans and unwittingly insult them and casually violate their ethics as well as their etiquette. Contrasts between Mexican-American and Anglo-American concepts of familial obligation and individuality, the roles of the sexes, honor and respect, achievement and acceptance are made clear. The system of folk medicine is given special treatment, with attention to disease entities and symptoms, treatment and theory, and particularly to native curing. The system is seen as self-maintaining and anxiety-reducing within the framework of conservative Mexican-American life. Excellent use is made of case data to illustrate and document all generalizations. The reader should be aware, as this case study is read, that the description is not intended as generalizable to all Mexican-American or Chicano populations in the United States. There are substantial regional and class differences. This is a case study of a particular population and locale.

In this second edition of this case study Andre Guerrero, who is introduced at the beginning of the Epilogue, writes about the confrontation between Chicanos and Anglos in the lower Rio Grande Valley, a part of the Chicano movement which began in 1966, two years after the first edition of this case study was published. William Madsen has provided a new introduction to the study as a whole.

GEORGE AND LOUISE SPINDLER
General Editors

Stanford, California
March 1973

Preface

The research for this study was conducted by the staff of the Hidalgo Project on Differential Culture Change and Mental Health during the four-year period from 1957 to 1961. The staff included: Antonieta Espejo, Octavio Romano, Arthur Rubel, Albino Fantini, and William Madsen (director). The project was financed by the Hogg Foundation for Mental Health, University of Texas.

Ethnographic field work took place in four communities of Hidalgo County, Texas, ranging from a rural-folk society of Mexican-Americans to a bicultural urban center. Names have been changed in this report in order to protect the identity of the informants. For the same reason, the names of the four communities have not been mentioned.

Invaluable material on the attitudes and value conflicts of the acculturated Latin came from the Spanish teachers who took my course on acculturation in the Foreign Language Institute for Native Speakers of Spanish (NDEA) at the University of Texas in the summer of 1962. I am most grateful to them for their perceptive insights into the process of acculturation.

This book was written while I was a fellow at the Center for Advanced Study in the Behavioral Sciences at Stanford University in 1962–1963. I am indebted to Benjamin D. Paul of the Stanford Department of Anthropology and my other colleagues at the center for stimulating exchanges of ideas about the subject matter presented here.

Acknowledgments are also due to: Robert Sutherland and Wayne Holtzman of the Hogg Foundation for Mental Health; George Sánchez of the education department at the University of Texas and other members of the Hidalgo Project steering committee; the staff of the Hidalgo County Health Unit; the many informants who contributed to our study; the photographer, W. R. Henry of McAllen, Texas; and my wife, Claudia Madsen, who assisted me in organizing the material for this book.

WILLIAM MADSEN

Contents

Introduction 1

1. The Magic Valley 6
   Spanish and Mexican Roots, 6
   Anglo Development, 7
   The Modern Economy, 8

2. Culture Conflict 10
   Plight of the Hyphenated Citizen, 10
   Spatial and Social Separateness, 11
   Cultural Images, 13
   Decreasing Discrimination, 15

3. *La Raza* 17
   World View, 17
   Focal Values, 19
   Prescribed Behavior, 22
   Proscribed Behavior, 23
   Leveling Mechanisms, 24

4. Immigration and the Lower Class 26
   The Land of Opportunity, 26
   Wetbacks, 27
   Braceros, 29
   Earning a Living, 31
   The Lower-Lower Class, 33
   The Upper-Lower Class, 34

5. Middle and Upper Classes 37
   The Emergent Middle Class, 37
   The Lower-Middle Class, 38
   The Upper-Middle Class, 40
   The Upper Class, 43

6. The Family and Society 46
   Family Solidarity, 45
   The Extended Family, 48
   The Nuclear Family, 49
   Marital Conflict, 50
   Parental Roles, 53

Growing Up, 55
Courtship and Marriage, 58

7. Religion 60
Interpretations of Catholicism, 60
Devotion to the Saints, 61
Protestant Proselytism, 64
Motives for Conversion, 66
A Case of Religious Change, 67

8. Sickness and Health 70
Supernatural Causation, 70
Pregnancy and Childbirth, 71
Theory of Balanced Relationships, 72
Classification of Disease, 73
Childhood Diseases, 76
Fright Sicknesses, 79

9. Witchcraft 82
Beliefs, 82
Identification of Witches, 84
Motives, 85
Treatment of Bewitchment, 86
Curers and Witches, 87

10. Curers and Physicians 89
Divine Election of Curanderos, 89
Modernization of Curing, 91
Relationships with Curers and Doctors, 93
Objections to Modern Medicine, 95
Increasing Reliance on Physicians, 96

11. Folk Psychotherapy 99
Resolution of Interpersonal Conflicts, 99
Value Conflicts of Acculturated Patients, 101
Social Outcasting and Reacceptance, 102
Treatment of Mental Illness, 106

12. Education, Politics, and Progress 108
The Language Barrier, 108
Lack of Goal Orientation, 110
Middle-Class Political Movements, 111

Epilogue by Andre Guerrero 113

Recommended Reading 123

Photographs on Following Page

Above: This rental unit is a typical low-income Latin-American wage earner's home. Although the exterior is unprepossessing, the interior is clean and orderly. Although sparsely furnished, it has a new television set.

Center: The home of an upper-middle-class Latin-American professional man in a well-to-do residential area. The owner is a second-generation Latin-American whose ancestors originally resided in Mexico.

Below: Latin-American men and women workers tend the moving belt, sorting and packing green peppers at a packing shed. It is not uncommon during the height of the packing season for a worker to do 12 to 16 hours or more. More work, more boxes, more pay seems to be his goal. He is fast, adroit with his hands and eyes, and does a monotonous job swiftly and efficiently all day long.

PEPPERS

El Valle de Todo un Poco
YERBAS MEDICINALES
R. APARICIO

BORDE
MISSION

Photographs on Preceding Page

Above: A United States border patrolman questions a group of wetbacks, while his fellow officer scans the opposite bank to see if any more of their compadres *will attempt to cross. (Courtesy the United States Border Patrol)*

Center: This typical Mexican-style herb shop sells religious paintings, medals, and household items. Individual paper sacks of herbs may be seen through the open doorway in the center.

Below: Evangelists of all faiths find a ready and willing listener for their preaching, as seen in this iron-covered building packed to the doorways for Sunday services conducted by Border Missions. This church, which is only two months old, is now filled each Sunday. The mobility of the church-goers is attested by cars parked along each side of the building.

Introduction

WHEN THIS BOOK was written in 1962 the United States had a vision of boundless progress. No problem was too great to be solved with American know-how and American dollars. As the most prosperous nation on earth, the United States intended to show the "backward nations" how to follow in her footsteps. It was an era of vainglory which would soon be shattered.

Our overseas efforts to promote progress, American style, made us extremely self-conscious about the lower living standards and foreign traditions of some minority groups within our own borders. In those days every American, regardless of ethnic background, was expected to share certain core values with every other American. These values included faith in America, science, and progress. Any group which did not display these three tenets of faith remained outside the mainstream of American life, especially if its members relied on a foreign language.

In South Texas, strenuous efforts were made to eradicate ethnic differences and remake the Mexican-Americans into 100 percent Americans. Despite the intensity of the Americanization program, it failed to produce much progress. To be sure, there were Mexican-American professional men who achieved success and acceptance in Anglo society. There was even a United States senator from Texas by the name of Henry Gonzalez. But the majority of Mexican-Americans remained in a subordinate position at the bottom of the economic ladder. Those who lacked skills and education worked in the fields picking crops for a pittance which Anglos would not accept.

Education was supposed to provide the key to progress but all too often it proved to be a demeaning experience for Spanish-speaking children who started school with little or no knowledge of English. Overwhelmed by an alien and hostile learning environment, these children frequently lost confidence in their own ability and dropped out at an early age.

Texas schools attacked the language problem by prescribing punishment for Mexican-American students who were caught speaking Spanish on the school grounds. When this heavy-handed strategy failed to produce the desired conformity, other approaches were tried. Anglo teachers urged Mexican-American parents to speak English in their home for the benefit of their children but the response was somewhat less than enthusiastic. The same kind of negative reaction baffled public health workers and social workers who tried to show the Mexican-Americans how to "improve" themselves by adopting Anglo ways.

All these well-meaning efforts rested on the assumption that anyone would seize a proferred opportunity to change toward the Anglo-American norm. On a competitive basis, the truths of formal education in school would overcome the "errors" of informal education in the home; the reliability of scientific medicine would eliminate reliance on folk curing; and the opportunity for self-advancement would increase individual initiative and weaken overdevotion to the cooperative family. To most Anglos, it was inconceivable that the Mexican-Americans might want to preserve their own cultural heritage. Just how wrong these assumptions were did not become clear to the Anglo public until the advent of the Chicano[1] movement.

Sometimes it was felt that the message of "the better life" was not getting through to the Latin population of Texas. In an effort to improve communication, one state agency undertook a reorganization which I was asked to evaluate. In

---

[1] The origin and meaning of the word "Chicano" are still being debated since it is not listed in Spanish dictionaries. The prevailing opinion seems to be that "Chicano" is short for "Mexicano" but the two words are not synonymous and many Mexican-Americans who refer to themselves as "Mexicanos" do not wish to be called "Chicanos." Although the word "Chicano" is not used in the standard Spanish of Mexico, it has long been known as a slang label for a certain type of Mexican characterized by low social and economic position. At the end of World War II, the Chicano label gained widespread usage in Texas where it was applied to Mexican wetbacks who came to this country as crop pickers.

Originally used as an epithet, the term has recently acquired new meanings, including the idea that a Chicano is a person of Mexican ancestry who will fight to defend himself and improve his position. Today the word means different things to different people in the Mexican-American communities of South Texas. In general, it has a positive meaning for young people who are proud to be called Chicanos but many of their elders still regard the word as a derogatory label. A recent survey conducted by the University of Texas Center for Communication Research showed that most Mexican-Americans in the Southwest prefer to be called Mexicanos or Mexican-Americans rather than Chicanos. Of the persons interviewed in Texas, Arizona, and California, only six percent preferred to be called Chicanos.

my opinion, the reshuffling of offices and interdepartmental relations accomplished nothing toward the goal of increasing rapport with the Spanish-speaking population. It seemed to me the task would be easier if Anglos knew more about Mexican-American goals and values. In particular, we needed to know the areas where change was desired and where it was not. I recommended that priority be given to a study of Mexican-American culture.

The gentleman who followed me with his own evaluation disagreed. Laying a friendly hand on my shoulder, he cautioned the audience against taking my advice: "To pay any attention to the primitive and superstitious practices of the Mexican-Americans would merely encourage them to continue their undesirable way of life. The best way we can help these people is to set ourselves up as Christian models for them to emulate."

Shortly after this conference, I received a letter from the Hidalgo County Health Department stating that it would welcome a research project on Mexican-American culture in that area. The Hogg Foundation for Mental Health agreed to sponsor and finance the study. Thus began the Hidalgo Project on culture change and mental health.

My purpose in writing this report was not to make generalizations about all minority groups or all Mexican-Americans. Rather, I have tried to describe the socio-cultural conditions of Mexican-Americans living in one county along the Mexican border. This book is not about the Mexican-Americans of San Antonio, Los Angeles, or anyplace else except Hidalgo County where proximity to the border creates conditions differing from those in other parts of the country.

In the following pages, I have attempted to provide some insight into the stresses of acculturation in Hidalgo County. By acculturation, I simply mean the process of learning a second culture. It is not the same thing as assimilation which means being absorbed and made alike. The loss of ethnic identity produced by assimilation does not necessarily occur during the acculturative process. Successful cases of acculturation have enabled the individual to function skillfully in Anglo society without renouncing his Mexican heritage or severing his ties with other Mexican-Americans. On the other hand, acculturation sometimes leads to assimilation for those who prefer an Anglo way of life. In order to illustrate the range of variation, I have supplemented my generalizations with case histories showing how acculturation affects the thinking and behavior of the individual.

Three levels of acculturation may be distinguished among the Mexican-Americans of Hidalgo County. The base line of the acculturative process is the traditional folk culture derived from Mexico but modified by its Texas setting. Strongly influenced by American technology and economic factors, Mexican-American folk society still retains core values of Mexican origin.

The second level of acculturation embraces individuals caught in the value conflict between two cultures. Born into folk society, they have acquired enough education and experience outside their own group to recognize the conflict between Mexican values learned from their parents and Anglo values learned in school. Some of these individuals learn to compartmentalize their lives, living by their parents' values on certain occasions and by Anglo values on others. On the same level of acculturation are those who consciously attempt cultural transfer in order to become a part of the dominant society. This transition is often marked by severe anxiety about cultural identity and group affiliation.

The third level of acculturation includes Mexican-Americans who have achieved success and status in the English-speaking world. Many of these individuals see science and progress as the twin keys to a brighter tomorrow. Some of them take pride in their Mexican heritage but others would rather forget it.

These three levels of acculturation often represent a three-generational process of change. Acculturative levels are further correlated with the class structure of Hidalgo County. In general, the traditional folk society consists of manual laborers who have been confined to the lowest level of the social, economic, and acculturative ladder. The intermediate level of acculturation occurs in the middle class where value conflicts are most keenly felt and solutions sought through adoption of Anglo ways. The highest degree of acculturation is found in the upper-middle and upper classes whose members often move with equal facility in the English and Spanish-speaking worlds.

To some extent, the three acculturative levels are merely conceptual constructs since the acculturation process occurs at all levels. Every Mexican-American in Hidalgo County cannot be neatly classified in one or another of these categories. Although value conflicts are most common in the intermediate level, they also exist in the other two levels. On all levels there is a strong feeling that the Mexican-American deserves the right to be a first-class citizen without renouncing his Mexican heritage. An eloquent expression of this desire came from a Mexican-American who sought the economic advantages of acculturation but opposed assimilation:

> I've worked for this country and fought for it. I would also die for it. But I want the right to be my own kind of American. I would no more renounce my Mexican heritage than the Anglos would renounce the English language. I am just as American as the Anglos but my ancestors came from Mexico. I'm a Mexican-American and I'm proud of it. We Mexican-Americans can contribute to the greatness of our country. All we need to do is organize, state our wishes, and vote.

Out of such sentiments came Mexican-American political action groups and the Chicano movement which offers its followers the chance to fight for rights still denied them in Texas. Some political victories have already been won but the battle for fair wages and hiring practices has barely begun.

There have been many changes in South Texas since the Hidalgo Project ended in 1961. The school system has instituted pre-school classes to prepare Spanish-speaking children for first grade. New programs of bilingual education have been inaugurated to promote literacy in two languages and to emphasize the bicultural heritage of Texas. Perhaps the most momentous event of the past decade was the birth of the Chicano movement during the farm workers' strike of 1966. To provide an inside view of the movement, Andre Guererro has written an epilogue for the second edition of this book.

1

The Magic Valley

Spanish and Mexican Roots

HIDALGO COUNTY lies across the border from Mexico in the valley of the lower Rio Grande of southeastern Texas. This fertile agricultural land embracing Hidalgo and Cameron counties has been known to some as the "Valley of Tears" but modern promoters advertise it as the "Magic Valley."

Seventy-five percent of the population of Hidalgo County is Mexican-American. These Spanish-speaking citizens consider themselves the true Texans and sometimes refer to the English-speaking residents as "foreigners." Their viewpoint has considerable historical validity because the Rio Grande Valley was originally settled by Spaniards and Mexicans nearly a century before the first settlers from the United States reached the area.

The Spanish government of Mexico initiated the colonization of the Rio Grande Valley in 1746 to protect Mexican towns from Indian raids and prevent encroachment from New France. Count José de Escandón was named conquistador of the new Spanish province of Nuevo Santander, which extended north and south of the Rio Grande. The first two colonies, Camargo and Reynosa, were founded south of the Rio Grande in 1749. Reynosa consisted of 43 families, an uncounted number of Indians, and 6000 head of cattle, sheep, and goats. Among the original settlers were a number of Spanish land grantees whose descendants still live in the Magic Valley. By authority of the Spanish Crown, the land-grant families became owners of huge haciendas where cattle and agriculture were introduced. Less prominent families received smaller allotments where they raised corn, beans, and squash. By 1800, the Spanish colony of Nuevo Santander contained 15,000 people and many more thousands of livestock.

After Mexico won her independence from Spain, the lower Rio Grande Valley became a part of the Mexican province of Tamaulipas. In 1836, Texas declared her independence from Mexico and designated the Rio Grande as the boundary between Texas and Mexico. However, Texas made no attempt to establish jurisdiction in the valley because the Spanish and Mexican landowners opposed a change in government and there were almost no United States settlers living in the area.

After Texas joined the Union in 1845, United States troops marched into the valley to enforce United States jurisdiction north of the Rio Grande. They met opposition from Mexican troops defending Mexico's claim to the land between the Rio Grande and the Rio Nueces to the north. When fighting broke out, the United States declared war on Mexico and the United States army invaded northern Mexico. To ensure victory, President Polk ordered General Winfield Scott's army to land in Vera Cruz. Scott captured both Vera Cruz and Mexico City in 1847. As a result of this defeat, Mexico ceded to the United States all territory north of the Rio Grande. By the treaty of Guadalupe Hidalgo, Mexican citizens living north of the Rio Grande had a choice between United States and Mexican citizenship. Some landowners returned to Mexico but most remained in Texas.

In the latter part of the nineteenth century, Europeans and American southerners came to the valley to conduct mercantile operations and settle on cheap land. These settlers were single men and many of them married daughters of the leading Spanish-Mexican families. Old-timers in the valley nostalgically recall "the good old days" when cattle roamed the grassy countryside and there was plenty of meat, corn, beans, and squash for everybody.

In those days, prestige came from south of the border. Upper-class Mexican-American families did not consider their daughters properly married unless the wedding ceremony was performed in Mexico with all the splendor of the Catholic Church. The bride and groom made the trip to Reynosa or Camargo in a carriage followed by a long caravan of stage coaches and men on horseback. Expectant mothers also crossed the Rio Grande to give birth in the more civilized surroundings of a Mexican town where trained doctors and midwives were available. Because of this custom, many Texas residents had Mexican birth certificates, which caused confusion when United States immigration regulations were enforced. Members of the old families take pride in the fact that they were born and married south of the border because these rites establish their ties with the older and more sophisticated culture of Mexico rather than with the crude culture of the American pioneers.

Anglo Development

The good old days drew to an end with the arrival of United States speculators from the north. These English-speaking newcomers were called Anglo-Americans or Anglos to distinguish them from the native population of Spanish-speaking settlers. The Anglos bought land from the Mexican-Americans for low prices by direct purchase or by bidding for land confiscated from Latin owners to cover unpaid taxes. In 1877, the sheriff of Hidalgo County sold 3027 acres confiscated from a Latin land grant to an Anglo-buyer for fifteen dollars.

The new Anglo-investors quickly realized that the potential of the valley could not be realized until adequate transportation existed for exporting the fruits of the land. Before the twenieth century, the valley was entered by stage-coach along the famous cattle trails or by steamboat up the Rio Grande. Hidalgo County contained no large communities and it was relatively isolated. Work on the first major railroad link with the rest of the United States began in 1903. The railroads opened the way for large-scale agricultural production. They also precipitated even more land speculation and an ever increasing inflow of Anglos. With the beginning of the twentieth century, Hidalgo County's economic and cultural orientation turned northward and the image of Mexico became that of a foreign land instead of a mother country.

By 1910, land investment companies had been formed and massive projects were underway to clear and irrigate the land. This boom in land speculation continued until 1930. Cheap labor was imported wholesale from Mexico to supplement lower-class Mexican-American labor in the arduous work of clearing the brush and digging irrigation canals. Refugees from the Mexican Revolution swelled the ranks of the Mexicans crossing the river. Many refugees were peasants but some came from the middle and upper classes of Mexico. During the Reynosa battle of 1913 between Pancho Villa's army and the federal forces of Mexico, streams of refugees crossed the Rio Grande with burros, caged birds, and all the possessions they could carry.

The mass immigration of Mexicans from the south was paralleled by an influx of Anglo land purchasers from the north and the middle west. Land companies offered free transportation to prospective buyers of farms and ranches in the Magic Valley. Many came and many bought.

The predominating relationship of Anglo and Latin was determined by these historical events. The land buyers were middle- and upper-class Anglos including businessmen, commercial farmers, professional men, and retired people. The Latins were mainly manual laborers. The Anglos tended to regard the Spanish-speaking population as part of the landscape that needed to be developed.

"When we came here, there was nothing but rats, cactus, mesquite, and Mexicans," stated an Anglo pioneer. The Anglos set about to change all that. They exhorted the Latins to exhibit industry, perseverance and sobriety. Progress had come to the Magic Valley.

The Modern Economy

Anglo financing and planning carried out by Latin labor transformed this remote outpost of Mexican culture into a prosperous and thriving area. Today the southern portions of the county are green with crops. Tall ornamental palms and citrus orchards relieve the flatness of the landscape. In the prosperous communities that line the highways, gardens are brightened by tropical flowers and tropical fruit trees such as the papaya and banana. Resorts and hotels boast of fine restaurants and large swimming pools to delight the midwestern tourists during their annual innundation. Across the river, Reynosa has prospered by the tourist trade too. In this Mexican city, the vacationing gringo finds curio shops, bullfights, bars, exotic venison and quail dinners, "family-type" nightclubs, strip tease parlors, and an impressive red light district known as "Boy's Town."

Although tourists constitute an important source of revenue, the economy rests primarily on products of the land. In the northern part of Hidalgo County, petroleum and oil are pumped from the earth. The Sal del Rey salt deposit has been worked from the earliest Spanish days. Cattle and sheep are still major industries. Above all, Hidalgo County represents a highly developed and rich agricultural land with fields of cotton, corn, beets, black-eyed peas, carrots, tomatoes, cucumbers, cabbage, green peas, potatoes, lettuce, onions, peppers, cantaloupe, and watermelon. But the most impressive crop is citrus fruit including red-fleshed grapefruit, oranges, and tangerines. At one time, Texas was among the three leading citrus fruit states in the union. The freezes of 1949 and 1951 severely damaged many of the orchards, however, and the threat of future freezes has led some growers to bulldoze their orchards in clearing the land for cotton planting. Cotton is one of the largest and most reliable crops of the county.

The growth of commercial agriculture was accompanied by the development of related industries. Canneries, packing plants, and cotton gins dot the landscape. Airplanes zoom in at frighteningly low heights to dust the crops. Trucks and railroads have a heavy seasonal business hauling products to distant markets. Stores carry on a brisk trade in agricultural machinery, fertilizers, and farm implements. Everyday necessities, luxuries, and amusements are provided by the usual business establishments including chain stores and movie houses.

Today the 1541 square miles of Hidalgo County support a population of over 160,000. One promoter of the Magic Valley has described them as 160,000 contented citizens. Some of these citizens are more contented than others.

2

Culture Conflict

The Plight of the Hyphenated Citizen

A CASUAL VISITOR traveling through Hidalgo County today could see little overt demonstration of tension between Anglos and Latins. Stores and restaurants welcome Latin trade. On the streets, Anglos and Latins exchange friendly greetings. One cannot fail to notice that some of the leading business and professional men bear Spanish surnames that are mentioned with respect in the newspapers.

The outward feeling of friendliness pervading the area may be illustrated by the experience of a Mexican-American friend of mine who came to the valley from California. He commented on the smiles and greetings he received from Anglo strangers. Experimenting with this Texas informality, he took the initiative one day and greeted a lanky Anglo wearing a Stetson hat and cowboy boots. The sour-looking Anglo broke into a smile and replied, "Why howdy son! It sure is nice of you to say hi to me." It took my Latin friend half an hour to disengage himself from the resultant conversation.

In many ways Texas is a friendly place but sometimes this friendliness masks areas of suspicion, distrust, and even fear between the two major ethnic groups. To a large extent, the mistrust accompanied by subtle discrimination is a matter of class rather than race. The majority of Anglos in Hidalgo County are middle class while the majority of Latins are lower-class manual laborers. Class differences reflect cultural differences that distinguish the Hidalgo situation from the class hostilities found in regions of a common ethnic background. The recognizable physical differences between Anglos and Latins accentuate their separateness. As one anglicized Latin said to me, "I think like an Anglo and I act like an Anglo but I'll never look like an Anglo. Just looking at me, no one could tell if I am an American or one of those blasted Mexicans from across the river. It's hell to look like a foreigner in your own country."

The Mexican-American who has had little education is even less identifiable as a United States citizen. In a border area, resembling a foreigner can be inconvenient. Pablo is a United States citizen born in Texas of Mexican parents. His dark complexion and Indian features indicate his foreign ancestry. He is a field hand who has never been to school and knows only a few hundred words of English. Pablo has a birth certificate to prove his citizenship but seldom carries it with him for fear of losing it. On several occasions he has been picked up by immigration officials on suspicion of illegal entrance into this country. Each time he has persuaded the officers to take him by his home so he could show them his proof of citizenship. Each time he was released immediately and once an officer apologized for the inconvenience. Another time, the officers drove him back to his job in the field. Pablo is not too bitter about these incidents but he does admit that they are embarrassing.

In the past, the Mexican-American resemblance to Mexican nationals has been dangerous as well as inconvenient, especially during crises between the United States and Mexico. Such a crisis period existed in 1914 when United States marines seized the Mexican port of Vera Cruz in retaliation for the Mexican military refusal to salute the United States flag in Tampico. Diplomatic relations between the two nations were severed. The Mexican-Americans of south Texas were frequently identified with the enemy just as loyal Japanese-Americans were suspected of traitorous potentialities during World War II. The Texas Latins were not interned but they learned to avoid the Anglo part of town if they disliked being involved in violence. The Anglos also found it advisable to stay out of the Latin community. A wall of fear grew between the Anglo and Latin communities. Recalling this period, a Mexican-American said, "All our people were afraid. And we were in our own country but the Anglos thought that we were not from here."

The plight of the Mexican-Americans grew worse when the Texas Rangers and United States Army troops entered the area to pursue revolutionary bandits from Mexico who were making raids across the United States border. Throughout the valley, gory sagas are told and retold about the "Hora de Sangre" —the Bloody Hour—when Texas Rangers reportedly shot innocent Mexican-Americans instead of the Mexican bandits they were supposed to be chasing. Some Anglos remember this period with shame. The Anglo widow of a prominent businessman commented, "All the Rangers had to do was get a suspicion on somebody, any little thing, and they would take 'em out and shoot 'em down."

Spatial and Social Separateness

The historical past is not forgotten despite the growing tolerance and friendliness in the valley. Incidents such as the Bloody Hour reinforce the barrier between Anglos and Latins created by differences in appearance, language, custom, and class. This division is both social and spatial.

The larger towns in Hidalgo County still maintain the planned geographical separation of Latin and Anglo populations initiated by the land development companies in the early part of the twentieth century. Today, each town and city is neatly divided into an Anglo and a Latin community. The dividing line is usually a railroad or a highway. Until the end of World War II, this boundary commonly served as effectively as an electrified fence to socially separate the two ethnic groups. Mexican-American entry to the Anglo side was restricted to employment situations or shopping expeditions. A Latin crossing the line at night was subject to police questioning or taunts and violence at the hands of Anglo teen-agers. Similarly, the Latin side of town was regarded as unsafe at night for Anglos, especially women. However, groups of Anglo males made occasional slumming trips to the Latin cantinas in search of beer and excitement.

The geographical division of the community is marked by speech differences. English is the predominant language on the Anglo side of town while Spanish prevails on the Latin side. The Spanish dialect of this region is commonly called Tex-Mex because it includes many hispanicized English words. Each side of town has distinctive labels. The Spanish-speaking population refers to the Latin community as *el pueblo mexicano* (the Mexican town), *Mexiquito* (Little Mexico), or *nuestro lado* (our side). They designate the Anglo section as *el pueblo americano.* The Anglos also refer to "our side" and "their side" and speak of the Latin community as being "over there." They generally designate the Latin side as "Meskin town."

The two sides of the tracks reflect the class differences between most Anglos and most Latins. Most Anglo homes are well-constructed and well-equipped with luxuries such as TV sets, washing machines, and air conditioning. They are situated in shady, well-kept yards. On the Latin side of town, homes are smaller and obviously of cheaper frame construction. Some are drab shacks with peeling paint, bare yards, and rundown outhouses. Others display fresh coats of paint in the lively pastel colors so loved in Mexico. Even the poorer homes maintain an appearance of brightness by decorating the yards with arrays of gaily-colored flowers neatly arranged in earthen pots or painted tin cans.

There is a noticeable difference in the pace, atmosphere, and noises characteristic of each side of town. The Anglo commercial area buzzes with the traffic din and the hustle of busy shoppers. The determined look of an Anglo housewife may be seen on the faces of women out to buy particular items of clothing in the near panic of a department store sale. People hurry along the streets with an appearance of definite purpose. Even coffee breaks are marked by the concentrated effort of purposeful conversation.

The Latin shopping areas lack the plush department stores of the Anglo side of town. Small stores sell produce, Mexican magazines, cotton clothing, or sundries. There may be a tiny hole in the wall specializing in medicinal herbs. The shoppers are more relaxed and there is more casual visiting. Pleasantries are exchanged between buyer and seller. From the cantinas come the strains of the gay-sad music of Mexico played on juke boxes. Traffic noises are less pronounced on the streets, many of which are dusty and unpaved. The Latin side is poorer but it seems gayer than the Anglo side. There are more children and dogs and more laughter on the Latin side.

Since 1946, the apartness of the two sides of town has been decreasing. Today, almost any Anglo neighborhood may have some Latin residents. In the evenings, Spanish-speaking families may be seen strolling to the movies in the Anglo downtown section. During the day, increasing numbers of Anglos go to Mexican town to eat enchiladas and tacos and drink beer. In one town, a Mexican-American judge settles complaints brought by Anglos and Latins.

Cultural Images

Despite the growing tolerance and intermingling between the two ethnic groups, each is still keenly aware of the differences that divide them. Feelings of resentment stem from a mutual lack of understanding and stances of superiority. Each group finds the other lacking in propriety of behavior and each feels superior in some respects. These attitudes are manifest in the labels by which each group distinguishes the other. Each group has polite terms for the other to be used in face-to-face contact and in press releases. These respectful terms include: Anglo, Anglo-American, Latin, and Latin-American. Anglos refer to themselves as Americans and use the term Mexican or Meskin for both the Mexican national and the Mexican-American. Depending on the particular usage, the term Mexican may be merely descriptive or derogatory. A decreasing minority of Anglos still use the face-slapping term "greaser" for the Latin citizen. Derogatory terms used by Latins to designate Anglos include: gringo, *bolillo,* and *gabacho.* Among themselves, Latins may refer to a respected Anglo as an *Americano.* Mexican-Americans[1] call themselves *tejanos* and sometimes speak of the Anglos as *extranjeros* (foreigners). Latins use the words *mexicanos* and *chicanos* for both Mexican-Americans and Mexican nationals.

Anglos reserve the racial term "white" for their exclusive use in the valley. This tendency is deeply resented by the Latins who see themselves lumped together with the Negroes as colored. The only similarity the average Latin sees between himself and the Negro is that they both belong to minority groups. Neither Latins nor Anglos have much direct contact with Negroes—who constitute less than one percent of the population of Hidalgo County. Until quite recently, the Negroes attended their own segregated schools. The Negro district in one urban center is often called "Niggertown" by both Anglos and Latins. Most Mexican-Americans say that they feel no hostility toward the Negroes but one Latin added, "Of course, I wouldn't want my daughter to marry a Negro." Negroes are almost never entertained in Latin homes.

There can be no doubt that the Anglo has a higher regard for the Latin than for the Negro. As an uneducated Anglo put it, "The Meskin's not a white man but he's a hell of a lot whiter than a nigger." Anglos regard the Latin

[1] Mexican-American and Latin are interchangeable terms.

field hand as superior to the Negro although they sometimes complain about the unreliability of the Latin. Many Anglos claim that the Latin is basically lax and unreliable but does a good day's work once he starts. An Anglo farmer pointed toward a group of Mexican-American crop pickers in a carrot field and commented, "They're all right if they have their own boss supervising them. Basically, they're lazy." This particular crew had been working at stoop labor for hours without a break. Another Anglo regarded Latins as the best of all farm laborers, "Man for man, a Mexican can out-plant, out-weed, and out-pick anyone on the face of the earth." Most Latins would agree with him. They think the Negro is too clumsy and the Anglo too weak to do a good day's work in the fields.

Anglos express different opinions on the Latin contribution to the development of Hidalgo County. Some say the area would still be a desert if it had remained Mexican. Another point of view was expressed by an Anglo rancher, "We've got to give them a lot of credit. They conquered the Indians and had ranches going here while much of our West was still wild." Perhaps the most common Anglo sentiment was voiced by a rancher, "If it were not for those hard working Meskins, this place wouldn't be on the map. It is very true about the Anglo know-how, but without those Meskin hands no one could have built up the prosperity we have in this part of the nation."

Although the Anglos fully recognize the economic importance of unskilled Latin labor, they tend to regard the Mexican-American as childlike, emotional, ignorant, and in need of paternalistic guidance. The American zeal for bettering people leads to the popular conclusion that the Latin should be educated and remade in an Anglo mold. At the same time, employers do not want to educate the Latin to the point of losing their labor force. The Anglo white-collar worker sees the educational upgrading of the Mexican-American as a threat to his job with the increasing employment of Latins in office and mercantile work at lower salaries.

The Mexican-American resents the economic dominance of the Anglo and his associated air of superiority. The Latin also objects to Anglo intolerance of Mexican-American ways and the pressures put on minority groups to conform to the American way. A Latin high school teacher summed up this attitude:

> The Anglo-American sees himself as the most important being that ever lived in our universe. To him the rest of humanity is somewhat backward. He believes his ways are better, his standard of living is better, and his ethical code is better although it is of minor importance. In fact, he believes that his whole way of life is the best in the world. He is appalled to find people on the face of the earth who are unable or unwilling to admit that the American way of life is the only way.

Many Latins believe that Anglos lack true religion and ethics and are concerned only with self-advancement. When one Mexican-American expressed the opinion that Anglos were not religious, another protested by saying, "Look at the number of people in their churches every Sunday." The first man replied,

"But have you looked at the altar? No crucifix. Only a bank book." As the conversation continued, a third man said, "The Anglo will do anything to get ahead, no matter who gets hurt. Of course, it's usually one of us who is hurt." A similar view came from the teacher quoted above, "Personal gain and achievement are the main Anglo goals in life and the ethics used to attain these goals will be worked out along the way." A Latin crop picker phrased the same sentiment in more transcendental terms, "The Anglo does what his greed tells him. The Chicano does what God tells him." He added somewhat hopefully, "I think that Anglos will be discriminated against in heaven."

The Latin feels that blind dependence on science and the ceaseless push for advancement have fettered the Anglo's integrity and intellectual ability. The Latin male sees himself meeting life's problems with intelligence and logic, which he finds lacking in the Anglo. An educated Latin pointed up the contrast in these words, "The Mexican-American has no disdain for thinking, no mistrust of it. He wants to arrive at his own convictions, do his own thinking. The Anglo-American will fit into almost any organization in most any way if he can only get ahead. He is often so overworked that even if he had faith in thinking, he would have little time for it. He accepts many facts although he does not understand them."

Decreasing Discrimination

Despite such unflattering images, the overt relationship between Latin and Anglo shows signs of improvement. Latins are well aware of the fact that discrimination is becoming increasingly rare. All can remember the days of segregated schools, direct insult, and unequal rights before the law. The Mexican-American sees the current change as a result of his efforts rather than a product of increasing Anglo democracy. "When we stand together for our rights, we will get what we should," is a common sentiment. The Anglo knows that when Latins do stand together they will control 75 percent of the votes. This realization makes Anglos more considerate of Latins.

Latins are listened to when they stand up to the Anglo now. Francisco advised a younger Latin to stand up and hold still in order to get the respect of the Anglo:

> We never used to do this. Instead we would take our hats in our hands and look at the gringo's feet. It was bad in those days before the war. The Mexicans suffered very much. They discriminated against us more than now. So, when the law came to make me go to war, I told them that before I was not good because I was Mexican. I was not treated as a citizen. Why was I good enough now to go to war? I told them I would go on not being good, just a Mexican. I said I wouldn't go to war. They went away and left me. Later I was a soldier and a good one. But I went to war because I wanted to. No Tejano runs from a fight. I went because I wanted to, not because anyone told me to. It pays to be a man.

As opportunities open for economic advancement and social acceptance of the Mexican-American, he still resists complete conformity to Anglo patterns. This resistance puzzles, and at times, angers the Anglo-Americans. Nevertheless, many Mexican-Americans are unwilling to abandon their cultural heritage from south of the border. The Latin pride in heritage was espoused by a college student:

> We're not like the Negroes. They want to be white men because they have no history to be proud of. My ancestors came from one of the most civilized nations in the world. I'm not going to forget what they taught me. I'm proud of being an American but I won't become a gringo. Now they're offering us equality. That's fine. I want to be equal before the law and have a chance to make money if I choose. But the Anglos are denying me the right to be myself. They want me to be like them. I want the chance to be a Mexican-American and to be proud of that Mexican bit. The Anglos offer us equality but whatever happened to freedom?

I asked the same Latin gentleman why the Magic Valley seemed so friendly when so much emotional hostility boiled beneath the surface. "I think," he replied, "that the Anglos smile at us because they need to be liked. We smile back because we're polite."

3

La Raza

World View

THE MEXICAN-AMERICAN thinks of himself as both a citizen of the United States and a member of *La Raza* (The Race). This term refers to all Latin-Americans who are united by cultural and spiritual bonds derived from God. The spiritual aspect is perhaps more important than the cultural. The Latin recognizes regional variations in behavior and realizes that custom changes. The spirit of the Spanish-speaking people, however, is taken to be divine and infinite. As one Latin expressed it, "We are bound together by the common destiny of our souls."

In Mexico, the concept of *La Raza* carries the idea of a splendid and glorious destiny. Mexicans see their greatest national strength in the spiritual vigor of *La Raza.* In Texas, the history of discrimination and economic subordination has modified the concept of the ultimate destiny of *La Raza.* Many Spanish-speaking Texans would say that God had originally planned a glorious future for the Mexican-American but it probably will never be attained. The failure of *La Raza,* he would continue, is due to the sins of individual Latins. Some believe that *La Raza* is held back by the sins of all Mexican-Americans, "The only ones among us who are surely free from sin are the little children." Other Latins think that only the worst sinners are holding back *La Raza,* "We could meet with God's favor again if the drunks and thieves would reform. We all suffer because of the sins of a few." I once asked a Latin if he thought the Anglos were in any way responsible for holding back the Mexican-Americans from their God-given destiny. "Of course not," he replied, "If we lived by God's commands we would be so strong that no one could block us. Of course, the Anglos take advantage of our weaknesses but it is we who make ourselves weak, not the Anglos."

The Mexican-American does not suffer undue anxiety because of his propensity to sin. Instead of blaming himself for his error, he frequently attributes it to adverse circumstances. The Latin does not think he missed the bus because he arrived too late. He blames the bus for leaving before he arrived. It is believed that everybody is subject to temptation under certain circumstances. Many succumb due to human weakness, which is a universal rather than an individual failing. Thus, Juan did not get drunk because he voluntarily drank too much. He got drunk because too much liquor was served at the party. The most common temptations that lead men astray are the opportunities to amass money or power. The main weakness of women is their inability to withstand sexual temptation. The safest course for the individual lies in avoiding exposure to a position where temptation is too great. In any case, the people of *La Raza* always suffer. Resisting temptation or succumbing to it can both be painful experiences. "Because we suffer in this world, we shall certainly be blessed with joy in the next," a laborer said.

In all aspects of existence, the Latin sees a balance of opposites. Pain is balanced by pleasure, life by death, creation by destruction, illness by health, and desire by denial. God maintains this balance by seeing that no extreme exists without a counterbalance. Pain must follow pleasure and a hangover must follow a drunk. God's ledger sheet is held to be exact and without error. Through creation and destruction, He maintains the balance of the world. He does not give life without death nor pleasure without pain. "One has to suffer to deserve," said Maria. It is a comforting philosophy for a subordinated group.

Suffering is also made acceptable by a strong belief in fatalism. It is generally believed that the good or bad fortune of the individual is predestined and every occurrence in human existence comes to pass because it was fated to do so. Fatalistic philosophy produces an attitude of resignation, which often convinces the Anglo that the Latin lacks drive and determination. What the Anglo tries to control, the Mexican-American tries to accept. Misfortune is something the Anglo tries to overcome and the Latin views as fate.

The Latin world view contains unpondered conflicts in the concepts of Divine will, individual will, and fatalism. Sometimes, events are explained as the result of the impersonal mechanism of fate, "What will be, will be." Certain individuals maintain that human fate is correlated in a mechanical way with the position of the heavenly bodies at the moment of birth. Others who accept the possibility of astrological divination point out that the course of the stars and planets is controlled by God. Most Latins believe that fate is a mechanism of God's will. Although the fate of the individual is decided before birth, God has the power to alter it. Through prayer, sacrifice, and even bartering, one can induce God to modify one's fate. The paramount nature of Divine will is reflected in the saying *Haga uno lo que haga, todo es lo que Dios quiere* (Do what one will, everything is as God wishes).

Unlike the Anglo world view where man emerges as the dominant force except on Sunday, the Latin view conceives of God as all-powerful and man as but a part of nature that is subject to His will. God enters all aspects of the Mexican-American's daily life and His name is used with familiarity. The name Jesús is still given to boys in the most conservative Latin homes. The Latin cannot understand why the Anglo considers this name amusing or sacrilegious when it is intended to show honor and respect to the Lord. The Mexican-American relationship with God was described in these words, "We see God in the beauty around us. He is in the water, the mountains, and the smallest of the plants. We live with God while the Anglos lock Him into Heaven."

It is sometimes said that the Latin works with God and the Anglo works against Him. The Mexican-American takes satisfaction in raising plants. He regards their growth and flowering as proof of God's will and beauty, while his own role is merely that of an attendant. One Mexican-American expressed his horror at Anglo attempts to create new botanical hybrids, "God gave us the plants to tend and admire and use for food. He did not intend for us to create our own. We should take things as they are given. Only God is the Creator." Another Latin fears the results of the probing of outer space, "We go too far," he said. "Now we are entering God's domain. We will arouse his wrath."

The Mexican-American world view was eloquently expressed by Don Luis, "We are not very important in the universe. We are here because God sent us and we must leave when God calls us. God has given us a good way to live and we should try to see the beauty of His commands. We will often fail for many are weak but we should try. There is much suffering but we should accept it for it comes from God. Life is sad but beautiful."

Focal Values

Acceptance and appreciation of things as they are constitute primary values of *La Raza.* Because God, rather than man, is viewed as controlling events, the Latin lacks the future orientation of the Anglo and his passion for planning ahead. Many Mexican-Americans would consider it presumptive to try to plan for tomorrow because human beings are merely servants of God and it is He who plans the future. The Latin lives for today instead of creating a blueprint for the future. He is dedicated to living the moment to its fullest in the roles assigned to him by God.

The most important role of the individual is his familial role and the family is the most valued institution in Mexican-American society. The individual owes his primary loyalties to the family, which is also the source of most affective relations. Gregorio said, "I owe everything to my family. Were it not for my parents' love for each other, I would never have been born. They raised me and taught me all I know. They have protected me and in my parents' home I know I will always find love and understanding. When one has a family, one is never alone nor without help in time of need. God created the family and one way to show respect to Him is to respect one's parents." The worst sin a Latin can conceive is to violate his obligations to his parents and siblings. Within the family, respect rests primarily upon the basis of age. The oldest male is head of the household and rules it. The old command the young and the males command the females. Latin society rests firmly on a foundation of family solidarity and the concept of male superiority.

The ideal male role is primarily defined by the concept of *machismo* or manliness. Every Mexican-American male tries to make his life a living validation of the assumption that the man is stronger, more reliable, and more intelligent than the female. He strives to achieve the respect of his society by acting like a "real man" in every situation. Perhaps the most common anxiety found in male Latin society is the fear of failure in the role of manly behavior. Next to devotion to the family, the male's "manliness" outweighs all other aspects of prestige. As one Latin male explained, "To us a man is a man because he acts like a man. And he is respected for this. It does not matter if he is short or tall, ugly or handsome, rich or poor. These things are unimportant. When he stands on his own feet as he should, then he is looked up to."

Machismo demands a high degree of individuality outside the family circle. It might appear that family obligations would conflict with a young man's need to be an individual and to stand alone. Actually, no conflict exists. The Latin male always represents his family and he must represent it with honor and devotion. In the outside world, he must tolerate no overt offense to his family whose honor he will fight to defend. As a representative of his family, he seeks to maintain its public image by becoming indebted to no one, acknowledging no obligations that might conflict with his familial role, and striving to achieve societal respect for himself as a man. Ideally, the Latin male acknowledges only the authority of his father and God. In case of conflict between these two sources of authority, he should side with his father. No proper father, however, would act counter to God's will for such behavior would make him less of a man.

The value of *machismo* governs male behavior in almost every facet of social life but wields its greatest influence in connection with the concept of honor. The conduct of a male in any social situation must support his public image as a person of honor and integrity. A situation that might compromise his image as a man of dignity is avoided. A Latin clerk commented, "Unless I am sure that I command the respect of the other guys in a gathering, I would rather not stick around. Only a fool would associate with those who look down on him."

Honor and respect are closely associated with lack of indebtness or obligation to those outside the family circle. For this reason, the Latin male is reluctant to ask for a loan or a favor. When he feels that circumstances require him to seek help from others, he tries to settle his accounts as quickly as possible. Anglo merchants and professional men are well aware of Mexican-American reliability in paying accounts. The Anglo who has done a favor for a Mexican-American friend has witnessed his earnestness in repaying the favor. "You are not whole and entire when you are indebted to another," Raul said. The more conservative Latins are reluctant to seek help from institutions because acceptance of charity is felt to be humiliating. It reflects on the head of the household who has failed to provide and thereby weakened the strength and solidarity of the family.

The obligations and loyalty involved in affiliation with formal organizations are regarded as a threat to the self-reliance of the individual and the self-sufficiency of his family. Unions, civic action organizations, and mutual aid societies consistently meet with failure in their attempts to recruit and hold membership from the male population of Latin folk society.

The concept of male honor requires the Latin to avoid being proven wrong. To take a stand on an issue and then retreat is regarded as degrading. Therefore, the Latin avoids openly stating an opinion unless he is ready to stand by it and defend it. When the Latin backs down from a stated opinion, he loses respect in the community. It is far better to avoid commitment on any issue than to risk being proven wrong. Involvement in controversial issues is regarded as foolhardy.

The manly Latin must repay an insult to himself or his family in order to defend the honor with which God endowed him. Revenge is usually achieved by direct physical attack, which may not be immediate but must be inevitable. The offended Latin may seem to ignore a minor insult at the moment but he does not forget it. A more serious offense may be met with a threat of future retaliation such as, "You will pay for this," or "We'll meet again." An open threat of this type must be carried out in order to maintain the *machismo* of the insulted individual. The act of revenge may take place months later and often occurs after an evening of drinking. The offender may be beaten, stabbed, or occasionally mutilated. Retribution settles the account but never restores normal relationships. The avenger has regained his honor but he does not forgive his enemy. The Anglo practice of shaking hands after a row is regarded as weak and unmanly.

Weakness is looked down on in all spheres of male activity. A man should be mentally and physically strong. Cripples are pitied but never regarded as manly unless their physical disability is compensated for by other strengths. Weakness in drinking ability is always humiliating. The true man drinks and drinks frequently and in quantity. Inability to maintain dignity when drinking is absolute proof of weakness as is the refusal to drink.

A favorite sport of the younger generation is testing the *machismo* of their fellows in a drinking situation. In this game, it is implicitly understood that hidden accusations and taunts are not serious. They are forgotten on leaving the bar unless some individual has gone too far or is too sensitive. An inebriated male is frequently egged on to make a stand that he cannot defend. His argument is then crushed with a well-turned phrase that is considered a triumph and a moment for hilarity.

Words and phrases with double meanings are used to insult the masculinity of one's drinking companions. Such verbal dueling may be developed into a fine art. The champions are those who can disguise their attacks with words of flattery so that the victim feels complimented rather than insulted. The possibility of taking serious offense limits verbal dueling to groups of very close friends. When the same disguised taunts are directed toward an enemy, a fight may result if the hidden meaning of the verbal thrust is recognized.

Male virility is better proven by direct action than by triumphs in verbal dueling. The Latin male does not take his sex life lightly. He regards the female sex as a desirable quantity that exists to be conquered, and he is the conqueror.

He is proud of the seductions he chalks up and does not hesitate to point them out to his companions. Seduction is the best proof of manliness. He regards prostitution as a pleasurable institution but rarely one in which he can prove his *machismo* except in an endurance contest. The only thing he proves by hiring a prostitute is his financial ability. This procedure does not call for the intelligence, strategy, and knowledge needed to seduce a reluctant female. The true man must demonstrate not only his physical prowess but also his power to lure women into sexual adventures.

Prescribed Behavior

The Latin thinks of a true man as being proud, self-reliant, and virile. He is jokingly compared to a rooster. Ramón observed, "The better man is the one who can drink more, defend himself best, have more sex relations, and have more sons borne by his wife. If unmarried, the better man is the one who has the most girl friends; if married, the one who deceives his wife most."

The Latin woman plays the perfect counterpart to the Latin male. Where he is strong, she is weak. Where he is aggressive, she is submissive. While he is condescending toward her, she is respectful toward him. A woman is expected to always display those subdued qualities of womanhood that make a man feel the need to protect her. A Mexican-American wife asked, "How can I expect a man for a husband unless I demonstrate my dependence on his strength?"

While the male feels compelled to demonstrate his sexual power with as many women as possible, the Latin woman must guard her purity above all else. A respected woman has had sexual experiences only with her husband. A loose woman is an object of jest and ridicule. Protecting the purity of a woman is no easy task in a community filled with males stalking their prey. Because women are regarded as weak, suggestible, and less intelligent than males, the purity of a female must be defended first by her parents and then after marriage by her husband.

The Latin wife is expected to show her husband absolute respect and obedience. For a wife to question her husband's orders or decisions is to doubt his intelligence—an unforgiveable sin. She does not resent her subordinate role nor envy the independence of Anglo women. Her role fulfillment is seen in helping her husband to achieve his goals as he sees fit. The Latin wife must never express sorrow or anger at her husband's extramarital activities. It is understood that his sexual adventures will not threaten or weaken his devotion to his family. The Mexican-American wife who irritates her husband may be beaten. She should accept this punishment as deserved. Some wives assert that they are grateful for punishment at the hands of their husbands for such concern with shortcomings indicates profound love.

Husband and wife share the joint obligation of teaching their children how to conduct themselves with dignity and honor in any social situation. In addition to serving as models, parents are supposed to instruct their children within the home and expose them to experiences outside the home that will prepare them for adult life. An "educated" person is one who has been well trained as a social being. Informal education within the family is viewed as more important than formal schooling.

The educated person displays polish and courtesy (*urbanidad*) in his social relationships. He knows how to avoid offending others and how to defend himself. He knows all the rules of Latin etiquette and the techniques for politely maintaining social distance outside the home. He respects his elders and conducts himself so as to receive the respect due him. In social interaction, he is expected to maintain a proper relationship with neighbors, friends, and acquaintances. Proper relations between members of *La Raza* involve ritual and respect patterns that are alien to the Anglo. Latin social relationships are highly formalized and life itself is seen as dramatic and ceremonial.

Proscribed Behavior

A person lacking urbanity may be characterized as inexperienced, for shortcomings are best blamed on circumstances. A discourtesy may be excused if the offender can be described as young and inexperienced. If this description does not fit, the impropriety may be interpreted as an insult or an offense. A child or young adult who violates tradition through ignorance rather than malice is called *tonto* (dumb or foolish). The implication is that the individual's shortcomings are due to lack of experience and will be overcome with maturity. The term is also applied to Anglos.

A proper relationship between experienced persons must preserve the dignity and individuality of each. Above all, one must not give offense to a friend or acquaintance. Polite social distance precluding direct involvement in the affairs of others is mandatory. Direct questioning of another's motives or methods may be taken as insulting, particularly if it is directed at an elder.

Direct criticism is also considered offensive. It is wrong to criticize the subjective beliefs of another person and even more inexcusable to try to change them. As long as a Latin conforms to the rules of proper conduct, he is entitled to his own beliefs. One may resent another's actions but not another's opinions or interpretations. This view is expressed in the Mexican-American saying, *Cada cabeza es un mundo* (Each head is a world unto itself). A person may think as he pleases but he should not try to impose his ideas on anybody else. These concepts of propriety are a major factor in the hostility felt toward missionaries and public health workers who are trying to change Mexican-American beliefs. A distinguished Latin citizen voiced his opinion on what he called "brain-washing," "Americans have abandoned geographic imperialism but to them mental imperialism is a wide open field."

To question the beliefs of another is to belittle him (*hacerlo menos*). A person also feels belittled when someone questions his accomplishments or compares them with greater successes achieved by others. When Memo mentioned the double he hit in a baseball game, he was offended that Pepe called attention to a home-run hit by José. The new mother of a baby girl was crushed when a friend asked her if she had seen Concha's baby boy, the third son in the family.

The most common way of belittling or abasing others is to attain greater social or material success than one's friends. To do so is dangerous for it may arouse the emotion of envy in others. It is considered prudent to conceal personal gains or advancement. Mexican-Americans value inconspicuous consumption as highly as Anglos value the conspicuous display of wealth.

Latins regard envy as a destructive emotion and admit that it is a major barrier to the material advancement of *La Raza.* Envy is felt to be such a powerful emotion that it is difficult or impossible to suppress. Sometimes, envy is so potent that it endangers the health of the person experiencing it. Envy also results in malice and hostility toward the person or family envied. A Mexican-American repairman explained:

> My people cannot stand to see another rise above them. When I rented my own little store, my best friends became jealous. When I painted my house, my neighbors thought I was trying to shame them. And after I purchased my new car several people stopped speaking to me. Every one tries to pull the one above him down to his own level. If you try to get ahead, you make enemies. If you don't get ahead you are criticized for laziness or stupidity. My people are hard to live with.

Envy may be aroused by success in almost any kind of activity. Josefina experienced envy when her neighbor bought new window curtains. Margarita felt envy and jealousy when her best friend married a highly desirable bachelor. Pedro resented Memo's success with the girls. A schoolboy experienced envy and anger when a classmate got a new bicycle. Envy occurs most commonly among neighbors, fellow workers, classmates, and other circles of daily contact. It is most strongly felt when an equal has made sudden gains and risen to a higher position. The tendency then is to try to equalize the position by pulling the successful individual down. While the Anglos try to keep up with the Joneses, the Latins try to keep the Garcías down to their own level. "We spend more time deprecating the success of others than in trying to improve ourselves," Pablo said.

Leveling Mechanisms

One leveling mechanism is gossip spread by the envious person about the individual who has gotten ahead of his neighbors. Gossip is considered improper behavior and frequent gossiping outside of the family circle can lower a person's prestige. Nevertheless, gossip is common. Criticism of another person is generally aired only in the family circle or in private, to a close friend. Because friendships overlap, the gossip spreads through the community in a remarkably short time and damages the prestige of the person involved. The person who starts the gossip takes pains to conceal his identity from the victim who would certainly seek revenge.

Ridicule is another leveling mechanism. It is used when only slight envy is felt. The ridiculing is done directly by a group of close friends so the victim will not pin the blame on any one of them. Such ridicule is usually gentle and often successful in removing the offensive behavior that aroused the envy. Pedro, a poor crop picker, saved his money to buy a fine suit at a department store. The day after the purchase he wore it to a cantina to drink with his friends. His magnificence made a sharp contrast with their drab and soiled work clothes. Immediately the joking began. "Pedro has come into money," Juan called, "the drinks are on him." Pepito asked if Pedro planned to run for mayor. Each jibe produced laughter but the general behavior indicated it was all in fun. Nevertheless, Pedro had an uncomfortable evening. The next night he came to the cantina in his work clothes. A few days later he quietly informed Pepito that he had given the new suit to his wife's brother who was getting married. No one believed his story but Pedro now looks and acts like his fellows in the bar.

Direct action may be taken to halt the advancement of the person envied. Two brothers who enlarged their cantina into a small night club were boycotted by their former friends. Several times the screens on the windows were slashed and the window frames broken. One night a truck "accidentally" rammed the wall of the establishment and the large crack had to be repaired at considerable expense. "We are doing a good business but our customers are strangers, not friends," one of the brothers said.

Witchcraft is the most feared leveling weapon of the envious. Failure in any undertaking may be attributed to witchcraft designed to reduce the victim to the level of his neighbors. Consuelo was unable to hold the well-paid job she had obtained in a large Anglo store because of her sudden and persistent headaches. She felt sure that somewhere a witch was tormenting the head of a doll made in her image.

Because a successful individual expects to be envied, he may imagine more hostility directed against him than actually exists. As a defense, he may begin gossiping about those whom he suspects of working against him. The defensive behavior of the upwardly mobile individual often creates as big a barrier as envy between him and his old friends.

The Mexican-American fears not only the envy of others but also their greed, dishonesty, and treachery. Early in life, he learns that he lives in a threatening and hostile universe. The motives of those outside the family are open to suspicion. The other fellow may be planning to belittle him or rob him. This cultural fixation enhances the value of social distance and further explains the reluctance to join organizations such as labor unions. The Mexican-American is taught to keep his defenses high. To drop them for a moment might give someone the opportunity to deprive him of what is rightfully his. He suspects both Anglos and Latins but believes that members of *La Raza* are most likely to yield to the temptation to do him in. He sees both his strengths and his weaknesses as part of his heritage from *La Raza* whose vision of a glorious destiny is blocked by wrongdoing.

"We are a people turned against ourselves," Roberto said. "The greatness God intended for us will never be ours for we are too busy devouring each other."

4

Immigration and the Lower Class

The Land of Opportunity

ADHERENCE TO THE PRINCIPLES of *La Raza* is by no means uniform. Conformity to these Mexican values depends on class pressures and exposure to Anglo influences, which in turn may be related to the length of family residence in the United States. In general, the value system of *La Raza* is strongest among the lower classes whose ranks are continuously replenished through immigration from Mexico.

The Mexicans and Mexican-Americans in Texas represent every degree of residential status. Some Mexican-American families have called Texas home since the time of the first Spanish settlements. Others became citizens after more recent migrations from Mexico. A few are aliens living illegally on this side of the border but posing as Texans. There are Mexican citizens who have resident permits to live and work in Texas. For years, there has been an annual influx of Mexican nationals who crossed the border to work as field hands. The wetbacks, who entered the United States illegally by swimming across the Rio Grande River, were followed by the braceros or *contratados,* who are Mexican laborers admitted to the United States under immigration treaties for seasonal labor. These legal Mexican harvesters, who are contracted to harvest United States crops, may vanish from the scene as a result of the 1964 termination of the bracero agreement between the United States and Mexico. Finally, there are the Mexicans who daily walk across the border to buy cheap merchandise in Texas chain stores.

Most of the Mexicans who came to Texas were economically motivated except for the refugees from the Mexican revolution. The majority of the immigrants were deviants in the folk cultures of Mexico where economic advancement of the individual is regarded as unworthy. A minority came from more sophisticated Mexican communities, which they abandoned in the belief that local labor conditions precluded the possibility of improving their financial position in the mother country.

Mexican immigrants seeking economic gain saw the United States as the land of opportunity. Wealth they had never known before was theirs. In the early days of Texas history, Mexicans crossed the border freely. It was not until the twentieth century that immigration regulations were enforced and the wetback era began. Although the inauguration of the bracero program reduced the number of wetbacks, illegal entry continued and still constitutes a major problem for the immigration department and the border patrol. The wetbacks and braceros returned to Mexico with possessions and tales of riches that inspired others to go north.

Wetbacks

While the bracero walked or drove across the international bridge, the wetback swam the Rio Grande or crossed by boat. During the harvest season when wetbacks crossed the river in droves, illegal ferry services were maintained at designated points along the Rio Grande. The fares were steep but the risks were high for the ferryman as well as his passengers. It paid to hire a well-known ferryman for some were thieves who stripped their customers of all clothing and possessions leaving them naked or dead.

The crossing was made at night on a flat boat, a raft, or a craft called "the duck" because of its peculiar shape. The duck was constructed of dried willow branches held togther with rope and the better ones were lined with canvas. As many as twenty persons could be accommodated in this craft. Single men often swam the river pushing a log with their clothing held above water. Some of the wetbacks never made the crossing. They were drowned or mysteriously shot from the American shore and their bodies were washed up on the river banks. Other crossed only to be turned back or jailed by the border patrol. In addition to the wetbacks, there were illegal immigrants called "aerialists" who entered western New Mexico and Arizona by climbing barbed wire fences. Some of the aerialists made their way into Texas.

Most of the wetbacks came to Texas only for a few months in order to make money picking crops. Some, like Alfredo, came to stay. Alfredo is a tall, handsome man in his fifties who proudly calls himself a Texan. He freely admits to his friends that he entered the United States as a wetback. "My determination to stay was great," he said, "fourteen times they caught me and threw me out but here I am."

Alfredo, who was born in Linares, Nuevo Leon, first crossed the Rio Grande in the 1930s on the duck with his wife and child. They entered Texas at night and slept in the brush. The next day he built a small jacal, a crude hut with a thatched roof and walls made of upright poles, covered with mud or clay, hidden by the mesquite so that his family would not be discovered by the authorities. Then he contacted Mexican-American friends who introduced him as a prospective laborer to an Anglo farmer. Once employed, Alfredo quickly demonstrated his competence in managing irrigation systems and became a trusted employee.

Whenever the authorities picked him up and deported him, Alfredo luckily was far from his jacal so his wife and daughter were not disturbed. He always returned the same night. Within two years, his wife gave birth to two more children with the assistance of a midwife who came to their hut. Friends helped register the births of these two children who are citizens of the United States. In time, Alfredo obtained a document from his employer stating that his services were needed due to the shortage of skilled agricultural labor in Texas. On the basis of this document Alfredo received residence papers and today lives openly and respectably in a small house in Ventura.

Alfredo's wife died recently but his citizen son and Mexican-American daughter-in-law live with him. He is proud of his two surviving children who have both completed elementary school. His son makes good money driving a truck. His daughter has married a Mexican-American laborer and has produced a grandchild for him. Alfredo likes Texas and says he would apply for citizenship if he could only read and write. "But if I marry again I'll get a Mexican wife from over there," he says, "these women here are spoiled."

Mexican-Americans have always demonstrated a willingness to help the wetbacks who come to Texas to stay. The local history of discrimination and violence against Latins make it natural for them to defend other members of *La Raza* from Anglo authority. Moreover, the wetback is respected for his courage. Crossing and remaining in this country illegally is a brave and manly undertaking. A resident who entered this country as a wetback may be kidded but in a friendly way. Sometimes when Alfredo enters a cantina, a friend reaches over to feel his shirt, "Just wanted to see if it is dry yet," the drinking companion quips. Alfredo laughs and takes no offense. Too many of his friends have come the same way to make an insult out of such a joke.

This type of jesting would be offensive and threatening to the uncounted illegal residents who have no papers. Most of these Mexicans work as field hands or at odd jobs. Some of the women work as maids in Anglo homes. An Anglo lady indicated her preference for Mexican rather than Mexican-American servants, "A Mexican maid without papers will really do her job without complaining. She won't want a day off either."

The Mexican who lives and works illegally in this country must constantly be on guard against apprehension and deportation by the authorities. He also must avoid offending a Mexican-American who might report him. When confronted by authority, the wetback customarily tries to brazen it out. "Look them straight in the eye," one advised, "only when you seem afraid will they know that you are from over there." Such play acting sometimes fails because of ignorance about the United States. One wetback stopped for questioning was asked where he was born. Standing proud and straight, he looked into the eye of the border patrol officer and replied "Chicago, California."

Braceros

Braceros have fewer problems because they enter this country legally. The Anglos like their labor and welcome their trade. The Anglo farmer is distressed by the thought that the bracero labor supply may be cut off but he comforts himself with the thought that rafts and ducks are still on the river and Mexicans can still swim. The Anglo merchant who received bracero trade remembers that the wetback who may be deported tomorrow is not a very good credit risk.

As a whole, braceros are not kindly regarded by Mexican-Americans. Latin merchants complain that the braceros take American money back to Mexico instead of spending it in Texas. The domestic field hand objects to Mexican nationals working in Texas because they threaten his means of livelihood. Thousands of harvesting jobs are filled by Mexican nationals who are often willing to work for less pay than the Mexican-American. Some Mexicans who originally entered Texas as members of a bracero group later obtained immigrant permits to reenter this country as permanent residents on the strength of job offers from their farm employers. A Mexican-American field hand describes his economic problem in competing with braceros and other Mexican nationals for jobs, "We used to earn about five dollars a day during the harvesting season here. Now, a farmer offers me three dollars or four dollars a day and if I refuse the offer he gives the job to a Mexican national. I can't support a wife and six kids on that kind of money."

Unlike the bracero, the Mexican-American must pay for his own transportation and fork over a kick-back to the crew leader in some cases. He does not receive the bracero's guarantee of employment or any of his fringe benefits such as free medical care.

When the braceros swarm into south Texas for the crop-picking season, the Mexican-Americans go north each year to harvest crops for higher wages. Only by this annual migration do some Mexican-American families manage to survive. In Illinois and Michigan, the crop pickers from Texas make a dollar an hour or more. Some of the families who go north or west settle there and abandon their Texas homes, which are rented or sold to other Mexican-Americans or to the new Texans coming out of Mexico.

Those who go north say they would prefer to remain in Texas. "This is our land," a Mexican-American said. "We made it and we love it. We don't like being pushed out by the braceros." Mexican-Americans also complain that many braceros are dirty and ill-mannered and these traits lower the esteem for all Latins in the minds of the Anglos.

The braceros cannot understand this hostility directed at them by Mexican-Americans. "How can they complain about Mexicans?" a bracero inquired. "Where the hell do they think they came from?" Actually, Mexican-American hostility is felt more toward the idea of imported labor rather than toward the individual bracero. The newly-arrived bracero may be regarded with suspicion but so is any stranger. When he is known, he is generally well-treated by Mexican-Americans who may even give him friendly advice on how to avoid being cheated and robbed.

Many braceros like Texas and decide to stay. A few return to Mexico and succeed in obtaining permanent contracts from United States employers who arrange for their resident permits. Others simply remain in the local Texas community without papers and try to make themselves as inconspicuous as possible. "I went through such hell to get here that I'm not going back," said a bracero named Juan. "I'm making fine money here and there are good ways to spend it."

The worst part of Juan's trip to the United States was his stay at the bracero enlisting camp in Monterrey, Mexico. Thousands of men from all parts of Mexico come here to get their names on the list of braceros who will be sent to the United States. Juan said:

> That place is like an insane asylum. Men are robbed while the mob pushes toward the enlistment tables and the loudspeakers warn about the dangers of being a bracero. All day long government officials shout through the loudspeakers warning the men not to carry money, not to listen to anyone offering contracts, not to attack anybody, and to be calm.
>
> Many of the men come to the enlistment camp from far away places like Oaxaca and the Sierra de Puebla. They have never left their villages before and they don't know how the contracting is done. They only know that they must pay to be enlisted. So they give their money to swindlers who carry notebooks and act like government officials. These crooks get all the money they can and disappear in the crowd when the authorities see them.
>
> The real officials who do the enlisting sit at a long row of tables out in the open where the men must show proof that they have done military service and are eligible to be braceros. When they get on the list they have to come back every day and listen until their names are called over the loudspeaker to go to the contracting office. Here they receive a permit to go to the border where they get their contracts.

"I've paid enough bribes to get here and I am going to stay," Juan concluded. He plans to marry a Mexican-American girl he met in Texas. "When she has had a couple of kids, I won't have any trouble. I'll go back to Monterrey and tell the American consul that I need permission to live in Texas to care for my American wife and kids." Juan does not want citizenship papers. He merely wants a resident permit to remain in Texas. "I was born a Mexican and I will die a Mexican," he said. "My kids will have it better than I did because they will be gringos but I want them to be able to say proudly that their father was a Mexican and that his blood flows in their veins."

If Juan's children are indeed born in Texas one day, their society will never allow them to forget that Mexican blood does flow in their veins. Thus, they will inherit membership in *La Raza* and thus they will be set apart from the Anglo community. As children of a Mexican crop picker, they will also be born into the lower class of Texas society.

Earning A Living

The Latin lower class first appeared in Texas with the arrival of Indian and Mexican peons who worked on Spanish ranches. In the twentieth century, the lower class was greatly expanded by Mexican immigrants responding to the demand for labor in land development. Today, as second and third generation Mexican-Americans move upward to the recently emergent middle class or outward to Michigan and California, the ranks of the lower class are filled by Mexican nationals seeking an economically richer life in the land of the Texan.

Mexican-Americans are not as class conscious as the Anglos nor are interpersonal relations as clearly structured by class among Latins as among Anglos. Nevertheless, lower, middle, and upper classes are recognizable among the Latins of Texas although they rarely use these terms.

The lower class earns a living by manual labor and constitutes the bulk of Hidalgo County's population. Members of the lower class are employed as agricultural laborers, food processors, cannery workers and servants but they are primarily associated with the land and its products. Mexicans and Mexican-Americans tend the fields, dig the ditches, and harvest the crops. They load, clean, and pack the fruits and vegetables. They tend, pick, and load the cotton for shipment to the gin and reload it for shipment to distant factories. They are an inevitable part of the daily scene in the countryside along the border.

The more fortunate members of the lower class have permanent jobs working for a respected boss on a farm or ranch. Most members of the lower class must depend on seasonal employment as field hands. They commonly join the crew of a Latin trucker who makes contracts with employers to deliver labor to the fields. The trucker receives all the wages and distributes the money to the workers. Each worker must pay the trucker a transportation fee of about fifty cents a day, which is withheld from his wages. If a trucker has good contacts with employers, he may also charge the worker a fee for joining his crew. Truckers are generally disliked for real or imaginary shortchanging of their crews. Mexican-Americans prefer to work for truckers to whom they are related.

Many Anglo employers pay crop pickers by the piece rather than by the hour. Piecework is measured in terms of bags, sacks, or boxes depending on the crop. The cotton picker is paid by the number of pounds he harvests. A good worker can make more money on a piecework pay basis than on an hourly basis. Experienced workers who are skilled in picking a particular crop can average as much as a dollar an hour on a piecework contract. The weaker and less experienced workers make less money on a piecework basis than they would on an hourly basis. Some male pickers reported that they averaged as little as thirty-five cents an hour when paid by the piece as compared with an average of fifty cents an hour when paid by time in the field. Women assert that they average only fifteen or twenty cents an hour on a piecework pay arrangement. Daily wages vary widely depending on the time spent in the fields. During the peak of the harvest season, Latins may work twelve or fourteen hours at a stretch. At other times there is no work at all.

Employers prefer men to women pickers because of the greater strength, skill, and endurance of the males. Mexican-American men avoid field tasks that yield extremely poor pay. These tasks are left for women and braceros. Weeding and carrot picking are among the jobs disdained by local males.

Many of the best Latin field hands prefer joining the migratory labor crews that harvest in other parts of the country. Some families make the trip in their own cars while others sign up with a trucker who arranges for their transportation, housing, and employment. These migratory workers say that they would be able to stay at home and work if it were not for the braceros but admit that they like the higher wages in the north and find the trip exciting. The Anglo employers in the Magic Valley say that the reason they have to import such large numbers of braceros is because the local Latins leave the area every year at crop-picking time.

Cannery workers can make more than field hands during the height of the harvest season. Some canneries pay twenty cents for each bucket of tomatoes and a good worker reports he can make up to eighty cents an hour. The Latin cannery foreman is distrusted and even hated. Mariana, a cannery worker who packs tomatoes, says "Those foremen don't care for their own people. They are always watching you to see that the gringo boss makes a good profit. The only cheating is done by the foremen." The foreman is given a nickname such as "the wolf," "the fox," or "the eagle," imputing a predatory nature.

Widespread dislike and distrust of truckers, foremen, and employers results in high job turnover. It is extremely common for Latin workers to feel that they have been cheated or insulted. For the slightest real or imagined offense, a Mexican-American may walk off the job or fail to turn up the next day.

One employment situation where true affection exists is in the relationship between the Latin maid and her Anglo mistress. A Mexican-American woman will not stay with an Anglo *madama* unless the relationship between them is cordial. In the close friendship that often develops between the two, the Latin servant turns trustingly to her mistress for counsel and aid whenever she is confronted by a crisis.

Lower-class Mexican-American women frequently supplement the family income by working as part-time cleaning women or taking in laundry or mending. Catering on festive occasions is another way for women to stretch the family funds. Margarita is a renowned cook who prepares dinners for the parties following Mexican-American baptisms and weddings. She is famed for her barbecued goat. Margarita sometimes makes more money cooking for one party than from two weeks of washing and ironing for Anglo women.

Lower-class Latin men sometimes find it necessary to seek supplementary work. They work in private homes as gardeners, window washers, floor waxers, and repairmen. During the off-season in agricultural work, they may take unskilled jobs in construction and maintenance work.

The means of livelihood and the aspirations of lower-class Latin families tend to divide them into two subgroups. This division is not verbally recognized by the Mexican-American and the boundary between the two groups is not well defined. Nevertheless, it is possible to speak with some accuracy of lower and upper segments of the lower class.

The Lower-Lower Class

The lower-lower class is composed mainly of immigrant laborers and first generation Mexican-American laborers in the towns and urban centers. In the *ranchitos* inhabited almost exclusively by Latin families, the lower-lower class embraces all generations and can be viewed as a class division only in relation to the broader social structure of the surrounding urban area. The lower-lower class is the stronghold of the folk value system of *La Raza*. The people of this class cling to the values of rural Mexico and have been less exposed to the pressures of anglicization than members of other classes. The lower-lower class has a relatively well-integrated culture that lacks the value conflicts of middle-class Mexican-American culture. The values and world view of the lower-lower class differ from those of folk Mexico only in two major respects: firstly, the Mexican-American is slightly more economically motivated than his Mexican counterpart. Secondly, the Mexican-American realizes that his affiliation with *La Raza* sets him apart from the dominant Anglo population instead of giving him a spiritual bond with the upper classes as is true in Mexico.

Money is viewed by the lower-lower class Latin as a means of fulfilling and enjoying his role in his own class rather than a means of changing his role or class. Uppermost in his motivations is the desire to live up to the dictates of *La Raza* and thus gain the respect of his fellows. His world is a Latin world and he avoids all unnecessary contact with Anglos whom he regards as threatening and incomprehensible.

Working the land seems to him to be a natural and noble labor. He is usually dependent on seasonal work in the fields. He takes jobs as they come and rarely complains to anyone outside his family about his pay or working conditions. He would prefer not to have his wife work but necessity may force him to let her help him in the fields. The environment of the canneries and packing houses is sometimes too alien and frightening for her to enter. The father regards his children as working members of the family and envisions their future as a duplication of his own life. For this kind of life formal schooling is unimportant except for the purpose of learning enough English to "defend oneself" against the Anglos and avoid being cheated in large stores or at work. Children leave school as soon as possible to obtain agricultural work and augment the family income.

Money is spent on necessities and those comforts that are compatible with one's place in life. The Mexican-American of the lower-lower class tries never to spend money in a way that would shame a neighbor or arouse his envy. Although most members of this class would like to own a home, few can manage it. Home furnishings are simple and luxuries are scarce. Extra money may be used by these deeply devoted people to buy pictures or images of saints and other adornments for the home altar. They rarely strive to accumulate money for the purchase of a new car or other luxuries beyond their means and the means of their equals. Life is seen as a fulfillment of God-given roles rather than a struggle for riches and power.

Pablo is a member of this lowest economic level of Latin society. He is twenty years old and lives with his illiterate parents in their rented, three-room house. He was born in Texas but his father came from Torreon, Mexico, and his mother came from Linares. His mother has never worked outside the home except for one season in the fields when her husband was ill. Pablo's father is proud that in normal times he can support his family without his wife's help. Their house is well cared for and they eat good food. Pablo's mother still makes her own tortillas and prides herself on her cooking.

Pablo attended school for five years and then left to work in the fields. His English is broken and only with an effort can he read the simplest articles in the newspapers. This does not bother him as he is not interested in the type of news that is reported in the local papers. He has worked in both citrus and cotton. Twice he has joined labor crews and gone north for the season. Most of his pay is turned over to his father to pay for his keep and repay his debt to his parents. His spending money goes for beer, cigarettes, and an occasional Spanish-language movie. He hopes to have enough money to buy a small house before he marries. Once he saved some money for this purpose but gave it to the church as a thanks offering after his father's recovery from a long illness.

When Pablo thinks of the future, he plans an evening at the cantina with his friends or the amorous pursuit of a girl. Sometimes, he sees himself driving an automobile—an ambition completely alien to his father. Pablo knows that his way of life will never provide him with the means to purchase a car. Occasionally he thinks about ways to enlarge his income so that his dream of owning a car might come true. Outwardly, Pablo conforms to the values of his class but his thoughts are beginning to parallel those of the upper-lower class. If Pablo ever buys his car, he may incite envy among his friends. He may then search out new friends who also own cars and do not believe that they are fated to follow in their fathers' footsteps. In this way, he would enter the upper level of the lower class.

The Upper-Lower Class

The upper-lower class strives for economic advancement and social advancement of the individual in contrast to the lower-lower class, which visualizes the future as a repetition of the past with perhaps a few more comforts or luxuries. The upper-lower class individual wants a better job, a larger house, a car, and a washing machine. Fate has a weaker grip on this individual who hopes his children will have it better than he has. He may even envision his children rising to the middle class.

The upper-lower class male is usually an agricultural laborer but he is often specialized in managing irrigation systems or handling farm machinery. He may abandon the fields for semiskilled labor in a factory or cannery, which pays a dollar an hour. He seeks steady employment in a year-round job. A good income is important to him and he is willing to let his wife work to supplement his earnings. If the family follows the migratory labor cycle, they probably travel in their own car instead of joining the crew of a trucker.

The head of the household still requires the labor of his children but he also sees the advantage of schooling for his boys. He tries to see that they finish elementary school and hopes that they may obtain a high school degree. He is not so interested in their grades as in their acquiring useful skills and abilities. Although Spanish is the language of the home, the father encourages his children to become fluent in English.

The members of the upper-lower class do not realize the extent of their anglicization. They would resent any suggestion that they are not good members of *La Raza.* Their homes contain the traditional family altar and their interpersonal relations are controlled by orthodox rules of respect and social ritual. Some of the behavior proscribed by the value system of *La Raza* is more noticeable in the upper-lower class than in the lower-lower class. In a subclass that values the products of an increased purchasing power, the individual tends to feel envy of his neighbors more than the member of the lower-lower class. He is careful to avoid exposing himself to the envy of others. A purchase that may set him too far above his friends is best kept out of sight. He remembers not to boast about advances in position. His weaknesses and failures are still blamed on the fate shared by all members of *La Raza.*

Antonio and his wife, Lupe, are members of the upper-lower class. They are making monthly payments on the purchase of the small frame house in which they live. For three years, Antonio has been employed as assistant gardener by a hotel that caters to the tourist trade. He takes great pride in the lawns and luxurious flowering plants that thrive under his care. He is pleased with his job and his pay although he thinks his boss fails to show enough appreciation of his work.

Lupe works in a cannery plant during the harvest season every year. While she is working, her teen-age daughter does the housework and takes care of a younger brother. The elder brothers work in the fields during the crop-picking season. Once they went on a cotton-picking trip to the north in the car of their first cousin. During the off-season in agricultural labor they take jobs as cleaning men and wholesale house employees. Both brothers say they would like to finish high school but feel they are too old now. One is sixteen and the other seventeen.

The combined family income is sufficient to meet the payments on the house and furnish it adequately. The kitchen has a second-hand refrigerator and a stove. Lupe is the proud owner of a washing machine. Their second-hand car is battered but shining and well serviced. Antonio has often thought of buying a new car but knows that his friends would regard it as pretentious. Most of them do not even own second-hand automobiles.

Lupe keeps the family altar in the living room decorated with fresh flowers. The central figure on the altar is a plaster image of Our Lady of Guadalupe. The Virgin is credited with saving the life of their daughter when she was ill with an acute case of "fright." Someday, Lupe wants the family to make a pilgrimage to the Basilica of the Virgin of Guadalupe in Mexico City to express their devotion and appreciation.

Antonio agrees with his wife that God and the saints have been good to them. He is a pious man who rarely gets drunk or chases after women. "I must be an example for my sons," he says. "If they work hard and do not offend God, someday they may own their own business and be dependent on no one." Antonio even contemplates the possibility that his boys might join *los de media* in the ranks of the middle class.

5

Middle and Upper Classes

The Emergent Middle Class

THE LATIN MIDDLE CLASS appeared in the Magic Valley during the Mexican Revolution with the arrival of a small group of refugees who had salvaged enough capital to establish themselves as tradesmen and farmers. This group remained small and insignificant until the end of World War II when Latin veterans initiated a remarkable expansion of the middle class, which still continues.

The returning veterans brought home army-acquired skills, ambitions, and decorations of honor. The refusal of a South Texas cemetery to accept the body of a Latin war hero attracted national attention and made Anglos realize that American ideals were being violated. Today, that hero is buried in Arlington National Cemetery. The crisis over his burial increased Anglo tolerance of Mexican-American efforts to gain recognition in the Anglo world.

Acceptance of Mexican-Americans was augmented by the returning Anglo veterans who had served alongside Latin soldiers and learned to respect them. "The war killed many of us but it gave us a better future," a Mexican-American veteran said. After World War II, Latin soldiers were treated as patriotic citizens when they joined United States forces serving in Korea and other overseas areas. Many of them were honored on their return to Texas.

Today, the growing middle class of Mexican-Americans is making an impression in the community. The financial successes and educational achievements of these Latin citizens command growing respect from the Anglo population but they also constitute a threat to the economic security of Anglo office workers. Latin secretaries and clerks who are as competent as their Anglo counterparts may be hired for less pay. Many Anglos who previously regarded the Mexican-Americans as a harmless part of the natural environment now see them as threatening competitors. New antagonisms and subtle forms of discrimination against Latin equals are developing.

The main characteristic of the Latin middle class is that its members earn their livelihood through occupational skills and the investment of capital. Although it is much smaller than the lower class, the middle class represents a far greater range of occupations including migratory labor contractors, store proprietors, small farm owners, mechanics, clerks, stenographers, and other white-collar workers. Except for the farmers, the middle class regards manual labor as degrading and a reflection of the lack of intelligence. The mark of middle-class affiliation is a white shirt and a suit worn in cool weather. Work clothes are never worn except by farmers and truckers when they are on the job. Increasing anglicization is reflected in the tendency to christen children with English first names.

Like the class below it, the middle class is divisible into two levels. The line of demarcation between the two levels is often difficult to discern and is recognized by the Mexican-American only in terms of those who are financially better off or worse off than he is. Social mobility and interpersonal relations are significantly affected by identification with the upper or lower levels of the middle class.

The Lower-Middle Class

The lower-middle class family usually owns a home and a second-hand automobile. Their skills or businesses make them less dependent on seasonal employment than the lower-class family. Economic advancement of the individual is an accepted goal but envy is extremely common. The individual wants a better income but resents an equal who gets ahead of him. The tendency is to pull such a person back "where he belongs."

A year or two of high school education is typical in the lower-middle class. Many members of this class have learned trades in school, military service, or apprenticeship. Some of them work for repair stores and maintenance shops while others are self-employed. Women frequently work as typists or beauty operators. Lower-middle class families rent and operate small stores without the assistance of outside employees. The truckers in this segment of the middle class usually own only one vehicle, which they operate themselves.

Manuel is the head of a lower-middle class family. He lives with his wife, Benita, and their four children in the Latin section of the growing city of Mecca. They own their home and have recently added a new room. They are proud of their Dodge, which is only a few years old. Manuel promptly repairs every dent and scratch on the car. He is a mechanic and works for a large automobile agency. He resents the fact that when he was ill, the Anglo who replaced him received a third more than his own salary. Manuel makes a few extra dollars by repairing machinery in the neighborhood during his spare time. Twice he has repaired the large fan in the grocery store.

Benita used to work as a clerk in a department store. She quit when their second child was born but still takes a temporary job during the Christmas rush. Before her marriage she worked as a maid in an Anglo home where she picked up ideas on home decorating and cooking that she uses occasionally in her own household. The pride of her kitchen is an electric mixer.

A conspicuous piece of furniture in their living room is the bookcase, which is almost unheard of in lower class homes. The books are the legacy of the children's education. There is also a book on the Korean war in which Manuel served as a United States soldier. He admits that he has never read the book but he likes to look at the pictures. A photo on the wall shows Manuel in his corporal's uniform.

The other pictures in the living room include photos of Manuel's parents, his son's high school graduation, and various religious portraits. The family altar is in the parents' bedroom. Here Benita kept a votive candle burning while her husband was in the army and while her infant daughter was ill. She cannot understand why their doctor rejected her diagnosis of the baby's illness as *caída de la mollera* (fallen fontanel). (The fontanel is one of the intervals, closed by membranous structures, between the incompleted angles of bones in a young skull.) He laughed at this diagnosis and called it superstitious. The family said nothing but they were deeply insulted by the doctor's rudeness and amazed at his ignorance.

Manuel and Benita completed two years of high school. Both are proud that their eldest son has a high school degree and was an outstanding football player. They hope their other children will graduate from high school too. Today, the eldest son drives a truck for a transport company but hopes to get a foreman's job in a packing plant. The other boys take part-time jobs after school but never work in the fields. They mow lawns in the Anglo part of town and one worked in a grocery store carrying customers' purchases to their cars. Manuel is gratified that they will never have to pick crops as he did in his youth. The money earned by the boys helps pay the installments on the TV set in the living room.

Manuel feels envy toward his neighbor whose son, Joe, is going to a local college. The neighbor has been cutting Manuel on the street since he heard that Manuel has been criticizing the way Joe runs around with girls and displays his knowledge of world affairs. Manuel says it is improper for the son of a "working man" to attend college and shame his neighbors by the accumulation of useless knowledge. In his own mind, he wishes he could send his eldest son to college.

Fidencio and his wife Virginia are also lower-middle class Latins. They live on a farm in a drab house with their two daughters. Fidencio has been planning to paint the house for several years but all his extra cash goes for seed, fertilizer, and farming improvements. He regrets that he has no sons to help him with the work. Both daughters go to high school but their father regards this endeavor as a waste of time. "What good is such knowledge to a woman who will be a wife?" he asks. "'Too much education gives a woman ideas that make it difficult for her to tend to her duties." One daughter thinks differently and dreams of becoming a nurse but she knows that her father would never consent.

Fidencio raises beans, carrots, beets, and corn. He is also raising pigs for a neighbor on a profit-splitting arrangement. The neighbor supplies the young animals, which are tended and fattened by Fidencio. When they are sold the neighbor will be reimbursed for the original cost of the animals, and the remaining profit will be equally divided between the two men. Fidencio feeds the pigs all the kitchen scraps and unusable vegetable products from the farm but he still has to buy extra feed for them. Nevertheless, he thinks he will make a good profit on the deal and plans to use it as a down payment on an adjoining piece of farm land.

He likes to hire a field hand to assist him whenever he can afford to do so. His wife and daughters help in the fields but he never mentions this fact to others. One day he hopes to own enough land so that he can hire a crew to take in the harvest. He thinks cotton would be more profitable than vegetables but doubts that it would be practical on his small holdings.

On Sundays, Fidencio puts on his suit and takes his well-dressed family to church in their pick-up truck. Their appearance gives no hint that they work on the land. About once a month they go to the movies in their dress-up clothes. Fidencio prefers Mexican films but also enjoys English Westerns and musicals.

Memo is a cab driver who may be classified in the lower-middle class. He lives with his widowed father and younger brother who is in high school. His father is a cook at a small restaurant. After school, the younger brother works as a bus boy and dishwasher in the same restaurant.

When Memo came back from the army, he kept on his uniform for several weeks so "people would not think I had been picking crops in the north." He sometimes feels nostalgic about his youth when he worked summers in the fields but he rarely discusses that part of his life. He would like to finish up the last year of high school needed for his degree but, being twenty-nine years old, feels that he would look too conspicuous in a "room full of kids."

Memo is a good cab driver and has regular Anglo customers who request his car when they call for a taxi. On the dashboard of his cab stands an image of Christ and pictures of saints adorn the visor. He is happy to render small extra services such as carrying heavy parcels for his customers. He also likes to chat with them. His favorite topics of conversation are baseball and the growing communities of the Magic Valley. When tourists riding in his cab ask his name, Memo answers that it is Bill. Someday, he hopes to own two or three cabs himself and thus become an employer rather than an employee. If he realizes his dream, he will be in the upper-middle class.

The Upper-Middle Class

The upper-middle class includes the owners of small businesses, highly trained technicians, and owners of small farms or ranches who employ a few field hands. The members of this class are separated from those of the lower-middle class by slightly greater economic means, skills, education, and anglicization. They are able to operate with more ease in nearly all areas of the Anglo world. Higher aspirations and a nearly universal respect for the value of higher education set the upper-middle segment apart from the lower-middle group. Envy is less common and the Latin custom of inconspicuous consumption may be replaced by the Anglo practice of conspicuous consumption. Here, the tendency is to try to keep up with a friend who is getting ahead instead of trying to pull him down.

Alberto is an upper-middle class Latin. He lives with his wife, son, and daughter in the apartment above his restaurant on the edge of the Mexican-American community, which is separated from the Anglo section by the railroad tracks. Alberto's restaurant has twenty booths and tables. It is rarely full except on Saturday nights when the field hands crowd in to eat and drink beer. An increasing number of Anglo male customers come in at noon for the fine Mexican food served by Alberto. A few tourists bring their families to Alberto's place for "real Mexican food" because they are afraid to brave the un-American germs that might lurk in Mexican restaurants across the river. Alberto appreciates his Anglo customers who spend more than the Latins and never cause any trouble.

He employs a waiter, a cook, and a dishwasher who helps him clean up. His daughter helps wait on tables during the noon hour and on Saturdays. Alberto and his wife alternately man the cash register. Both of them check the kitchen frequently to see that the food is being prepared correctly and that no one is loafing. Alberto suspects that his help steals food from the kitchen. The employees do not think that Alberto treats them with sufficient dignity. Their last waiter quit after being criticized by Alberto's wife in front of some customers.

Above the cigarettes and candy bars on the shelves behind the cash register hangs a framed picture of St. Martin and his horse. From time to time, Alberto's wife places a glass of water with some grass in it before the picture for the horse. When she forgot to do this one week, there was a fight between some young men in the restaurant. She is afraid they lost some regular customers as a result of her negligence. Alberto laughs at her concern about the horse's well-being.

Alberto and his family are good church members who attend early mass every Sunday before they open for business. He is keenly aware of his duty to worship the Lord and he wants to maintain his respectability in the community. By the cash register, he keeps a small coin box with a plea for customers to donate to a Catholic charity.

Although he never finished high school, Alberto prides himself on his knowledge. During slack periods of business, he reads both English and Spanish newspapers. He owns a World Almanac and likes to consult it for facts during discussions with close friends. He maintains that if the Mexican-Americans would pull themselves together they could gain respect and control the local elections. However, he refused to vote for a Latin political candidate who "spent all his time with Anglos." "He's forgotten he's a Mexican," Alberto said. "I don't know if we can trust him."

Alberto's son, Pedro, is in his second year at the local college. Alberto is sometimes criticized for buying the boy an old car and allowing him so much freedom. "He's my son and I'll do all I can for him," Alberto said. "'He's an American and he should act like his buddies in college." He encourages his son to bring his Anglo college friends to the restaurant for dinner. Once Pedro did this but he was ashamed when his mother waited on the group and his father attempted a joke that seemed immature. He was even more humiliated when some Mexican-Americans at the counter began to show their beer and mouthed obscenities. Pedro explained to his friends that the revelers were "just braceros on a toot." He does not want his mother to know that his school friends often call him Pete.

Despite his father's wish for him to take over the family business, Pedro never wants to have anything to do with the restaurant. When he obtains his college degree, he wants a "good job in business." He is not sure how his literature major will help him but he is sure that he doesn't want to spend the rest of his life serving food to "a bunch of loud-mouthed Mexicans."

Alberto was distressed to learn that his son had twice dated an Anglo girl. He had a long talk with Pedro about it and was upset because his son seemed to resent his advice. Alberto's daughter has never been on an unchaperoned date and Alberto wants his son to marry a girl who is "pure." "It's all right for a young man to fool around but what a scandal if he should get an Anglo girl in trouble," Alberto said. Pedro cannot understand his father's belief that any girl who will spend the evening alone with a man is immoral. He also resents the fact that several Anglo girls have refused to date him.

Alberto wants Pedro to marry María and has mentioned this subject to his son several times but the response has not been enthusiastic. In Alberto's mind, there are many reasons for thinking that the two young people would make a good match. María has been protected and her mother has trained her well in the arts of cooking and housekeeping. She is "modern" like Pedro and holds a high school degree but she does not act like some of the rowdy Anglo girls. She knows her place and she never argues. Pedro does not dislike María but finds her unattractive and uninteresting. He describes her as one who "doesn't know her way around."

Her father, Jorge, owns a small grocery store and news stand not far from Alberto's restaurant. He sells many Mexican imports ranging from dried chiles to Mexican magazines and carries a large stock of medicinal herbs. The store seems cluttered to the Anglo eye and it smells strongly of spices and fruit. Jorge works behind the counter but he also employs a clerk and a part-time clean-up boy. In addition to his income from the store, Jorge makes extra money by hauling produce in his own truck for other merchants and small farmers. He realizes that his friend, the restaurant owner, is a step above him on the economic ladder so he approves of the proposed match between María and Pedro.

Jorge regrets that his own son and daughter-in-law have moved to

Michigan where the son works in an automobile plant. He scarcely believes that his son could be making the salary he writes home about. "He probably exaggerates a little," Jorge said. "And, of course, he has to give some of his salary to the union. I don't know why he lets those union people blackmail him out of part of his pay every month. But, of course, they are Anglos." Jorge is thankful that he still has his daughter at home and thinks she has been raised well. "She will make a good wife," he tells Alberto. "She is refined and well behaved. She will never be like that Flores woman."

Anita Flores is definitely upper-middle class but conservative Mexican-Americans disapprove of her. After finishing high school and a course in a beauty school, Anita married a Latin college student and worked for two years to put him through school. Shortly after the birth of their son, in 1942, her husband was drafted and later killed in action. She has not remarried.

A year after her husband's death, Anita used his GI insurance money to buy the small beauty shop she now operates in an Anglo shopping area. At first, she worked alongside the other operator she hired. Now she has three assistants and only works on the hair of old and favored customers. All of her customers are Anglos as are many of her friends. She lives in an apartment on the Anglo side of the tracks and shuns the Mexican-American community. In the evening, she attends lectures at the college and once a week she goes to the meetings of the woman's club to which she belongs. No one has heard her speak Spanish for years. She has even changed her religion and today attends a Protestant church.

Anita's son, John, has been well educated. He and his mother always speak English at home. Although he can converse in Spanish, he quit using that language during his junior year in high school. He had few Latin friends in high school but was quite well accepted by some of his Anglo schoolmates. Today he is an outstanding student at the University of Texas. He plans to enter medical school after obtaining his B.A. degree. John seems destined to embark on a successful career as a member of the upper class.

The Upper Class

The Mexican-American upper class is small in numbers but its members are extremely influential. While the Anglo associates the upper class with economic power, the Latin associates it with personal power to command authority. A few upper-class Latins command both authority and wealth. Some have either one or the other. In the folk society of the Mexican-American ranchito where there is no upper class, prestige status is accorded to older men who have earned the title of "Don" by living up to the ideals of *La Raza.* This honorific form of address is also bestowed on a few Anglo employers who command the respect of the Mexican-American community.

The true elite of Latin society in the Magic Valley are the descendants of the Spanish land grant families. "They have owned the land since the beginning," said a middle-class Mexican-American. "They are the real Texans and they are gentlemen." They are indeed gentlemen who hold to the old European tradition that wealth in itself is meaningless unless it is accompanied by an honorable family tree and the refinements of a "cultured life." Family is valued above wealth by the Latin elite. Some of the older families live in genteel poverty while others have maintained, enlarged, or gained fortunes. A man's influence, irrespective of money, rests on his family and his ability to live up to the role he inherited.

The elite are clannish and associate freely only with their equals who are widely and thinly distributed throughout south Texas. Many of them maintain close connections with branches of their families in Mexico whom they visit frequently. Some wealthy families in Texas have large holdings in land or industry south of the border.

The elite think of social stratification in terms of caste rather than class or nationality. They look down on other Mexican-Americans as peasants, tradesmen, and upstarts. The elite are friendly to upper-class Anglos but regard them as boorish, ignorant, and lacking in manners. During a conversation with a wealthy Anglo, a Latin aristocrat made a subtle jest using the symbolism of Cervantes. When the Anglo looked confused rather than amused, the Latin said, "Of course, you have read Don Quixote." The Anglo brightened and replied, "No, but I saw the movie." The Latin later shrugged and commented to a friend "What can you talk about to such people outside of cotton and the comics"?

The Mexican-American elite are devoted Catholics who are loyal to the church. They send their children to parochial schools and the better private colleges. Some are sent abroad to universities in France. Their university education tends to focus on the humanities and the arts until they enter graduate school. The most highly valued graduate degree is in law. Practical considerations are drawing some members of the younger generation into business and medicine where they frequently desert the traditions of their elders for a successful career in the Anglo world. The older generation feels threatened by this trend. In time, some say, the days of the great families may be found only in books and memories.

The young rebels from elite families are identifying more and more with the wealthy Anglos and the upper-class Mexican-Americans who have achieved their status through vertical mobility. These "self-made" Latins of the upper class include the owners of large business establishments, important ranchers and farmers, and professional men such as lawyers and physicians.

Newly-arrived members of the upper class are hesitant to admit their lower or middle class origins. They are frequently ashamed of the poverty and superstitions of the Mexican-Americans. An eminent physician of the Latin upper class vehemently denied the existence of folk curers and witchcraft belief among the Mexican-Americans of the Magic Valley. He would be more comfortable in an area where he is not reminded daily of his lower-class ancestors and his link to *La Raza.*

Paul, the son of an upper-class Latin lawyer, has a degree from business school and is in business today with two Anglo partners. He is doing very well financially. Socially, he is seeking complete assimilation in the Anglo world. He belongs to a good club and attends parties in Anglo homes. Outwardly, there appears to be no question of his acceptance in Anglo upper-class society. Privately, however, he admits to his Anglo wife that he often feels his apartness from his Anglo partners and friends. He says he can feel their antagonism although there is never any overt manifestation of hostility. He has the feeling that he is being ridiculed behind his back. Sometimes, he tells his wife, one of his partners puts an arm around his shoulder as he explains a prospective business contract but while he talks, he winks at the other Anglo partner as if to say "We'd better put it in pretty simple words for this peon." It is impossible to say to what extent such condescending behavior actually is directed against Paul and to what extent he senses nonexistent insults.

The Mexican-American who has made it into the upper strata of Anglo society is still sensitive and afraid to relax his defenses. He often feels great bitterness about his ancestry and identification with *La Raza.* When Paul came home from college on a vacation one time, he told his mother about a real or sensed insult he had received from a professor about being a Mexican-American. "I wish I could get every drop of Mexican blood out of my veins and change it for something else," Paul said to his mother. "I'd take any blood in the world. Anything except Mexican"! His children will have only half of his complaint because their mother is an Anglo.

6

The Family and Society

Family Solidarity

THE FAMILY IS THE MAIN FOCUS of social identification in all classes of Mexican-American society. Only with the most anglicized Latins does individual desire become a more powerful motivating force than concern for the family. The upper-class rancher and the lowly crop picker both think of themselves first as family members and secondly as individuals. Mexican-American society as a whole classifies the individual first as a member of a particular family and secondly as a person with certain talents and shortcomings. "One is thought of first as a García or a Cantú and second as a Raul or a Marîa," a Mexican-American explained.

The family is a sanctuary in a hostile world full of envy and greed. The Mexican-American child who has been humiliated by Anglos at school knows that he will receive love and understanding from his mother. The wife who has been abused by her husband can seek help and guidance from her parents. Any Latin boy with a brother knows he need never stand alone in a fight. As long as one member of the family has a house and food, none of his close relatives will lack shelter or meals. Looking back on his early family life, an educated Latin recalled, "Our home was like a mighty rock in a stormy sea. It was fun to swim and fight the waves. It was also fun to return to the rock. It was a remarkable rock. It could even reach out and pluck you from the sea as you were going down."

As the family protects, so it demands. Every individual is regarded as a walking symbol of his family. He can increase community respect for his family or drag it into the mud by his behavior. To bring shame on one's family is an unforgivable sin. If the shame is great, the family may sever relations with the individual. When Lolita was sixteen, she was arrested by the police for soliciting on the streets of Chapel. She was found guilty and sent to a juvenile reform school. During her incarceration, no one in her family answered her letters. After her release, her father barred her from the house and forbad the family to speak to her. Nevertheless, her mother secretly arranged for her to live with an aunt in another city. Her father blames his wife for bringing up Lolita badly. When he is drunk, he beats her and accuses her of producing Lolita by bedding another man. His other daughter is now supervised every minute of the day and night. The father feels that his family could not remain in the community if it had another scandal. As it is, he is sure that most of the gossip in the neighborhood is about Lolita and the weaknesses in the family that she exposed. He is correct in this assumption although no one would openly confront him with the family disgrace. An elder brother once overheard an acquaintance making a lewd joke about Lolita. The joker was so badly beaten that he required hospitalization.

Anglicized Mexican-Americans sometimes regard the conservative Latin family as the main obstacle to advancement. A university graduate said, "It's only a miracle that I went to a university. We had the money because my father has a good job with the county but I wanted to go to the University of Texas in Austin and that's a long way away from home. My mother and my sisters said they couldn't stand it without me for four years. My father was afraid I would disgrace myself. Moreover, I was frankly afraid to go off on my own but I did."

A Mexican-American high school teacher thinks that the conservative family is preventing the development and recognition of individual abilities that would help elevate the Latin community. Speaking of the Latin family, she said:

> Granted that it is a beautiful, warm, and comforting institution, it is still carried too far sometimes. My sister had a beautiful voice and she had the chance to accept a fellowship to go to New York for study and training. But our father had to consult with his brothers and sisters, all ten of them, and the decision was that New York was too far away and too full of dangers for a young girl so a great talent went to waste.

The same teacher says that family obligations prevent the economic success needed for advancement in this world. "I like the concept of a strong family," she asserted, "but many a young couple is kept broke because relatives in every degree of kinship feel free to descend on them at any time and the food bill is very high. This is no exaggeration. I've been through it."

Conservative Latins regard such criticism from the more anglicized younger generation as nearly blasphemous. Fidel Rivera complained of his son's ambition:

> He wants to move to California where he says he can be on his own and get ahead. What kind of a life is that? He says he is tired of contributing to the family and he doesn't need it. Just wait until he gets into trouble. Then he'll come crawling back. And if he goes out there and stays, what will happen? Someday he will die and be buried there. When he goes before God, He will ask, "Who are you?" Fidel will say, "I'm a Rivera!" But God

will answer, "That cannot be so. You are not buried near your parents nor did you help them when they were old!" God made the family and when you turn your back on it, you offend Him.

Today the Anglo value of individualism is in direct conflict with the Mexican value of family solidarity in the Magic Valley. The Anglos believe that equality in the home and self-advancement are necessary to maintain the American ideals of freedom, democracy, and progress. Mexican-Americans believe that putting family above self is necessary to fulfill the will of God. In the process of acculturation, the Anglo ideal of the democratic family is slowly breaking down the Latin family, which is the main stronghold of *La Raza.* The Latin family is strongest today in the lower class and it is fighting to preserve its identity in the middle class. The traditional strong family of the Latin elite is losing ground as the more anglicized members of the upper class attempt to combine individual mobility with a strong family unit. Regardless of class affiliation or degree of anglicization, the ties of the Latin family are far stronger than those of the Anglo family.

The Extended Family

The nucleus of the Mexican-American family consists of parents and their offspring but the bond between parents and children extends over three generations. Because the family name and affiliation are traced through the father, the paternal grandparents are generally of more importance than the mother's parents. The ideals governing the relationship with one's grandparents were summed up by Gilberto, "As I respect my father, so I must respect and obey his father whom he regards as head of the family. As I love my mother, so I must love her mother and respect her father. All my grandparents, in turn, love and care for me for am I not the son of their children? We are bound together by common blood and our souls are joined together throughout eternity." Whenever possible, each household in the extended family is located near the others. It is a common sight to see two or more houses of related families crowded together on one piece of land in the lower-class districts.

As the grandparents are respected and obeyed, so are the parents' brothers and sisters. Uncles and aunts are well known and frequently visited. First cousins are almost as close as one's own brothers and sisters. The ties with more remote relatives are maintained when possible although they are never as close as those mentioned above. Mexican-Americans think it is wonderful to have many relatives and keep in touch with them. Migratory labor trips are an occasion for visiting relatives in other parts of the country. It is common practice to plan the itinerary so as to include communities where relatives live. Such trips are doubly rewarding because they produce both economic gain and the opportunity to renew familial bonds. Having kin at one's destination further assures help in case of need.

The range of kinship is extended beyond genetic links by the institution known as *compadrazgo* or coparenthood. *Compadres* (coparents) are sponsors who assume carefully defined roles in relation to the other participants in a religious ceremony establishing ritual kinship. The most important *compadres* are the baptismal godparents of one's children. The parents and godparents become *compadres* who are linked by tradition through interlocking obligations of mutual aid and respect. The relationship is formal and dignified. Proper *compadres* address each other with the formal *usted* rather than the informal *tu* pronoun. One is never supposed to gossip or joke about his *compadre.* In any kind of trouble, *compadres* have the right to call on each other for help and advice. They are expected to visit each other regularly and cultivate a close relationship.

The godparents of a child's confirmation rank next in importance as *compadres* of the child's parents. It is not uncommon for baptismal godparents to also serve as confirmation godparents. The *compadrazgo* relationships established at weddings are not regarded as significant. It is customary for the best man to become the groom's *compadre* and the maid of honor to become the bride's *compadre.* Other occasions that used to require *compadrazgo* ceremonies are becoming increasingly rare. The old custom of choosing *compadres* for the blessing of a new house has nearly vanished.

Parents try to choose *compadres* who are respected, honorable, and good-hearted. It is considered bad taste to choose a *compadre* of higher social and economic status than oneself. Such a choice is regarded as an indication of scheming and ambition to rise above one's neighbors. It is becoming increasingly common for *compadres* to be chosen among relatives, such as aunts and uncles. The reason given for this practice is that *compadres* who are not genetically related to the family may move away from the community to a new location where they are unable to fulfill their obligations as godparents. It is said that one's own family stays together or at least travels far to fulfill the duties of godparenthood. Having *compadres* who are blood relatives also strengthens the bonds of the family that is threatened by increasing anglicization.

The Nuclear Family

The nuclear family preserves its integrity within the extended family by maintaining a separate household occupied by the husband, the wife, and their children. When a parent of one spouse dies, the surviving parent may join the home but this situation almost always leads to a conflict in roles and a division of loyalties.

When Raul's widowed mother moved in with him and his wife, turmoil followed. Raul's wife described the situation, "Before his mother came to live with us, all was peaceful and regulated. Now, no one knows how to act. I used to prepare the meals as was proper. Now, my mother-in-law tries to tell me what to cook and how to cook. She says I waste money on food and then she demands that I improve the quality of the dishes. The other night we went to a movie together. I wanted to see that new musical but she insisted that we see the Cantinflas movie. She had her way." Raul explained why he decided to take them to the Mexican film, "What could I do? My mother who raised me had asked to see it. It made my wife mad and I'm sorry but she has no claim on me. I married her but my mother birthed and suckled me. My mother's blood is in my veins. But we were happier before she came to live with us."

Within the home, interpersonal relations are ideally dictated by rules of decorum and respect. Frivolity and disrespectful behavior are threats to the structure of family relationships. Sex and age determine the role of each family member. Authority rests with the males who are ranked by age. The effective members of the family are the females who receive respect that can be measured by their years. "The father should be obeyed," Rogelio said, "and one's love for his mother should be demonstrated by respect and devotion."

While the Mexican-American male may be a second-class citizen in an Anglo-dominated world, he can be a king in his own home. He is entitled to unquestioning obedience from his wife and children. He is above criticism due to his "superior" male strength and intelligence. Whoever enters the home is expected to acknowledge the husband's authority within that setting. No visitor is ever expected to enter a house or be seated without a specific invitation from the head of the household. As a guest, the visitor must follow the conversational leads of his host and avoid the expression of independent opinions. To a large extent, the supremacy of the male within his own home compensates for the subservience he may have to demonstrate on the job or in the presence of a social superior. *En mi casa yo mando* (In my house, I command) is the byword of the Mexican-American husband no matter who gives the orders outside of his home.

The wife is expected to give comfort and pleasure to her husband. She must acknowledge his authority and superiority and think of his needs before her own. She is supposed to accept abuse without complaint and avoid resentment of his pastimes and extramarital affairs. Her in-laws may criticize her and her husband may beat her for demanding that he spend too much time at home.

She sets the tone of the home atmosphere, ideally by radiating love and understanding. In her role as wife and mother, she is frequently compared with the Virgin of Guadalupe. This holy model for female behavior possesses all the most prized values of womanhood: purity, sanctity, tolerance, love, and sympathy. By extension but rarely by direct comparison, the husband and father is seen as a human image of God. He is aloof, absolute, and forceful in administering justice.

Marital Conflict

Although behavioral goals are based on divine paragons, the Mexican-Americans take cognizance of their human frailties. "Man was made in the image of his Lord but while God is perfect, man is full of weaknesses and imperfections," a Mexican-American husband said. The husband-wife relationship is rarely a blissful acceptance of divinely inspired roles. Marital conflict often results from the male desire to prove his *machismo* outside the home.

The young husband must show his male acquaintances that he has more sexual energy than his wife can accommodate. To prove his prowess, he often continues the sexual hunt of his premarital days. He may demonstrate his physical and financial resources by visiting Boys' Town with his drinking companions after an evening in a tavern. The most convincing way of proving *machismo* and financial ability is to keep a mistress in a second household known as a *casa chica.* Few men in the lower class can aspire to such luxury, which constitutes the height of manly success among middle and upper-class husbands.

Mexican-American society maintains a system of checks to prevent the male from threatening his home life with extramarital adventures. Foremost is the community's expectation that a husband will not allow any activity to interfere with his obligations to his wife and children. If the welfare of his family diminishes as a result of his sexual activity outside the home, the husband must face social disapproval and the intercession of his in-laws. His behavior damages his reputation in the community and brings dishonor on his parents. Exaggerated dedication to sex at the expense of friendship also demonstrates a lack of intellectual ability in social interaction. A third check on extramarital excesses is fear of the venereal diseases defined by modern medicine and the folk disease called *mal de sangre* meaning bad blood. The latter disease is defined as contamination of the blood caused by excessive carousing. It is said to produce deformities in the fetus.

A man who picks up a sexual disease and infects his wife is degraded forever. Pepe is still paying the price for committing this sin. His wife left him to return to her parents' home. She blamed him for the deformity of their infant son who was born shortly after Pepe contracted the disease. Pepe's own father no longer welcomes him for, he says, "my own son has contaminated my blood that flows in my grandson." Pepe is openly mocked by his friends who often greet him with an obscene gesture symbolic of the disease. They tell jokes about Pepe "who can only lure sick women to sleep with him." These insults are too common for Pepe to attempt revenge on anyone but himself. Today he is an alcoholic and his *machismo* is nonexistent.

Sexual promiscuity on the part of the wife is a heinous crime. So fragile is a woman's purity, according to Mexican-American belief, that one sexual indiscretion inevitably leads to a life of complete sexual abandon. No man would remain with a promiscuous wife unless he is already so debased that nothing matters. Reynaldo is such a man. At an early age, he served a prison term for assaulting his own father. As a result, his parents and their kin no longer acknowledge his existence. His excessive drinking interferes with the employment he needs to provide money for liquor. Quenching his thirst is more important to him than sex or respectability so he allows his wife, Flora, to have a generous Anglo lover. Flora maintains this illicit relationship partly to punish Reynaldo for his failings. Her shame about her promiscuity leads her to give her husband most of the money she receives from her lover. The sense of degradation that Reynaldo suffers from accepting this money makes him so angry at himself and his wife that he frequently flogs her. So unusual and outrageous is the behavior of this couple that they are cited as an object lesson of what happens when men and women forget their proper roles and fail to master their weaknesses. One of their neighbors expressed it this way, "The Holy Family is a divine example of how we should live. God allows such people as Reynaldo and Flora to exist to show us how far we can fall."

Most married couples fall far short of the divine model but never approach the sordid depths of Reynaldo and his wife. Marital problems caused by sex are meager compared to the conflict in roles brought about by growing Anglo influences. The husband's authority and the wife's submissiveness are both changing in response to the Anglo example. In general, the role conflict is weak in the lower-lower class and begins to emerge in the upper-lower class. It is primarily a middle-class phenomenon. Both the elite and the liberal upper class have worked out more clearly defined roles than have the partially-anglicized Latins in the middle segment of society.

Throughout the class structure, Mexican-American women gossip among themselves about how they are abused by their husbands. Wives who have been influenced by the Anglo example often try to improve their subordinate status by seeking an equal voice in decision-making. It is difficult for the male to compromise his authoritative position because doing so involves a lowering of his self-esteem. The result is marital conflict.

Serafín is a happily married man of the upper-lower class who views with alarm the changing female role. In his home, there is no friction over decisions. He follows the tradition of male authority, which is fully respected by his wife. But his son, who lives in a nearby community, distresses him. He says:

> Why that boy never stands up for what is right! I just don't understand it. Whenever there's a decision to be made he runs and asks his wife what she thinks. Of course he's doing all right financially so he's not dumb. He works in a bakery and can afford things I never had. So why does he put up with this nonsense? He makes the money and it's his house but he doesn't run it. She does. It's a disgrace!

Some husbands do not take kindly to wives who demand a say in family decisions. A middle-class electrician gave this picture of his home life:

> My home is not my own. Now my uncle is a man I admire. He consults no one and his wife is humble and obedient. My woman! Lord but she gets me down. She questions my word and is always demanding this thing or that. I have no peace and my kids laugh at us when we fight. Sometimes, I belt the woman and she shuts up for awhile, but not for long. I don't know whether men are getting weaker or women are getting stronger.

The more old-fashioned Latin women likewise look at the new "democratic wives" with horror but also with amusement. A wife from the upper-middle class commented:

> If these younger women were more feminine they would never have to demand. They would get what they want the way I do and I lack nothing that my husband can give me. When I need something from my husband I don't demand it. I encourage him to think of giving it to me by himself. Men like to please their wives. It makes them feel bigger. When I wanted a new sofa I only mentioned that Pablo must be making fine money because he had just bought new furniture for their house. I said that I didn't want them to visit us for they would be comparing our furniture to theirs in their minds. My husband often feels envy toward Pablo. The next day he told me we should fix up the house a bit. I not only got the sofa. I also got a new chair and a lamp. I tell you these emancipated women don't know anything about men. When a man has to defend himself against you, you get nothing. When he has to protect you, you get everything.

The conservative Latin wife is, in fact, a skilled manipulator of her lord and master. The weapons she uses in disguised form are his own self-esteem, his *machismo,* and his role as provider and protector.

Parental Roles

Children in the more traditional families learn early in life that their mother can influence their father in strange and subtle ways. A Latin teacher said, "When the children are in trouble, they tend to seek the mother's aid. She is the bridge to the father." As a wife, a woman's primary obligation is to please her husband. In her role as a mother, she is responsible for the well-being of her children. She sees that they learn what is expected of them and cushions the hurts that go with growing up. She frequently seeks the counsel of her mother, sisters, and other close female relatives on the problems of child raising.

The father sees that the children stay in line and punishes transgressions. He often sees his role as that of policing the family to preserve its public image as an integrated and honorable unit. He holds himself responsible for the behavior of individual family members both within the home and in society as a whole. He constantly judges and punishes those who fail to live up to his expectations.

The relationship between parents and children is relatively permissive during the period of early childhood. The exception occurs in lower-lower class families where children may be assigned exacting household tasks while both parents work in the fields. The small child is regarded as an *angelito* as yet uncontaminated by human sin and error. He receives adoring affection from mother and father alike. The father may drop his dignity to cradle a child, care for his needs, or even crawl on hands and knees to play with him. Such behavior is confined to the home.

The authoritative role of the father in relation to the child becomes clearly crystallized only with the onset of puberty and "reason." Then, the father withdraws from his position of doting parent and playmate to that of the dignified master of the home. He avoids demonstrations of affection and demands that the child show him respect. Younger generation Latins who are more anglicized than their parents often resent the absolutism of the traditional father. Mexican-American college students asked to evaluate the Latin family felt that the father's role was too authoritarian. "It is true that the children have a great respect for the father but it is a respect based on fear," one student said. Another stated that "the father should not always play the role of a tyrant. He should be a friend to his children, not a dictator."

At the same time that the father appears to the child as the aloof enforcer of proper behavior, the ties with the mother are strengthened. The close affective relations between parents and child are now usually limited to mother and child. A teen-ager described this relationship, "When I have problems I first go to my mother. She sympathizes and understands. If I went to my father he would upbraid me for having gotten into the problem in the first place." Another teen-ager said:

> My father has no sympathy. When I was eleven some other kids ganged up on me and hurt me bad. I went crying to my father. A big help that was! The old man slapped me in the face and said to quit crying like a woman. The only time he didn't hit me or ridicule me for tears was at my brother's funeral. I learned that my mother can feel sympathy but my father only demands and demands and demands.

Taking problems to the father may be an admission of misbehavior that is usually avoided. Some problems are not proper to take to the mother. "Sinful" behavior must be concealed from her to avoid offending her purity. It is also assumed that she lacks the experience to advise on many worldly problems. To request such advice would imply that she had experience in areas that no proper woman knows about. A mother's purity is a precious thing and anyone who questions it risks violence.

While the father is obeyed and the mother is adored, both are entitled to great respect. Frivolous behavior is to be avoided in their presence. The proper son or daughter does not smoke, drink, or engage in flippancy in front of his parents. The only occasion when it is proper for anyone to drink intoxicants in the home, except the father, is when he invites others to take a drink in celebration of a special occasion.

The slightest expression of anger by the father is usually sufficient to put a stop to improper behavior in the home. The same results can be achieved by a mother's threat to "tell your father." Either parent may administer a spanking or a few cuffs to children under the age of ten. Such punishment at that age usually is administered only for flagrant disrespect or behavior that might endanger the child's life. When the children are older, either parent may punish a daughter but a son is disciplined only by the father as a rule. He may punish minor offenses by ordering the boy to spend a few hours at manual labor in the yard "to help you remember who you are." In the case of serious offenses, the son may be beaten.

A son who "made a fool of himself" by the unmanly behavior of indulging in loose gossip about a female cousin was ordered to do his sister's household chores for a month "to see if you really enjoy acting like a woman instead of a man." This punishment was considered particularly degrading and humiliating. When Josefina, a high school student, asked her mother to obtain her father's permission for her to go to a movie with a date, the mother slapped her repeatedly while asking God if her own daughter was destined to be a whore. The indignant mother repeated the request to her husband who threatened to lock the girl in the house until she learned to control her passions. The next day, the girl's mother was very gentle to her and bought her daughter a new scarf. That afternoon the mother accompanied her daughter on a visit to the home of her aunt where the conversation somehow focused on a "loose girl" who had sinned and was now held in contempt.

Brothers and sisters are punished for failing to show respect to each other. Marta remembers well what happened when she and her sister got into a fight over the possession of a handkerchief. She was twelve years old at the time. Her parents stood the two sisters in the yard facing each other and tied each of them so they could not move their legs or left arms. A whip was put into the right hand of each girl. "Now have it out," the father said. "Whip the girl you hate until you are no longer angry." Marta recalled that they were both shocked at first. "Then we began to giggle. When we were laughing hard, my parents joined in. My sister and I never fought again."

Growing Up

Ideal relationships between mother and daughter and between sisters are especially close partly due to the female tendency to group together in a male-dominated world. The closeness is reinforced by the custom of pulling daughters more tightly into the home at the onset of puberty in order to protect their purity. The teen-age daughter of a traditional family stays home and helps her mother with the housework after school and on weekends. Her most constant companions are her mother and her sisters. She is never allowed to be alone with a boy. Her girl friends are often relatives or family friends who visit each other's homes. During her teens, the daughter is expected to acquire the graces of social interaction within the home and develop her talents as a cook and housekeeper. She prepares for her future role as a mother by helping to care for the younger children. In the event of her mother's sickness, the eldest daughter is expected to take charge of all household tasks.

Restraints on the behavior of teen-age girls are relaxed in anglicized families to the disgust of the more conservative Latins. There are families in the middle and upper classes who are reluctantly allowing their daughters to date without chaperones, although this practice has not penetrated the ranks of the elite. "It is indeed scandalous to allow these children to be tempted," said the wife of a grocery store employee. "One is powerless in the face of passion so what can you expect when a girl and boy go off together? Soon virginity will be as unknown among our unmarried girls as it is among the Anglos. God forbid that I ever allow my girl to become a plaything for some young beast. Better she were dead!"

The case of the teen-age boy is different. It is during his teens that he becomes a man and this transformation takes place outside the home. The boy approaching manhood spends most of his free time with male friends away from home. His closest contacts within the home are with his brothers. He protects his younger brothers and seeks advice from his eldest brother. Brothers are supposed to stand together in time of trouble and form a protective group for their sisters. Although a brother may tease his sister, he tolerates no disrespect for her from an outsider. The relations between brothers are determined by age. The older brother must be obeyed and treated with respect. During the teens, the relationship between brothers becomes formalized so that they no longer play together or joke with each other. Pablo expressed his attitude about this relationship, "I respect my older brother above all other young men. How can I, in turn, receive his respect if we joke and horse around together? When we talk, it is of serious things. Among my friends, I sometimes call him my 'little father.' " When Pablo's father dies, the eldest son will, in fact, take his place as head of the family. If the "little father" then marries and sets up a new household, Pablo will in turn take command of the home.

The respect patterns governing the relationships between brothers result in association with different sets of friends outside the home. Mexican-American youths tend to form loosely-knit play associations known as *palomillas.* The word means moths that, like the young men, cluster in groups around a light in the early evening. *Palomillas* lack formal organization and leadership and the membership may be constantly changing. The size of membership varies from two or three individuals in one *palomilla* to as many as 25 in another *palomilla.* The average number is eight or nine. The group is held together by common interests and the pleasure of social interaction.

The *palomillas* of younger teen-agers engage in sports or explore new activities. Unlike the juvenile gang, the *palomilla* does not claim a territory that it must defend. Its members are more interested in what goes on within the group than in testing their strength against other groups. Although some *palomillas* give themselves names, this practice is rare. Affiliation with a particular *palomilla* is not recognizable by distinctive dress or mannerism. Group affiliation may be terminated at any time by simply absenting oneself from group activities. It is even possible to belong to more than one *palomilla* at a time.

Although a young man's closest relationship with a group outside the family is with the *palomilla,* he does not discuss intimate and confidential matters with all its members. The hostility of the world can penetrate any group but the family. Fellow members of the *palomilla* may be buddies today but a careful man realizes that they may be enemies tomorrow. It is best, therefore, to reveal no unusual weaknesses or secrets. The need for a trusted companion usually leads to the development of a very close friendship with one other member of the *palomilla* who is known as an *amigo de confianza.* These two close friends come to know more about each other and share more adventures than they experience elsewhere outside the family.

Within the *palomilla* made up of younger boys, discussions take place in vacant lots or other secluded places. When the boys are older, beer parlors become the favorite gathering places. Sports are a popular topic of conversation for the young Latin is extremely interested in ball games and the athlete is often his hero. An equally popular subject is sex. As sex instruction within the home is rare, boys learn its terminology and techniques by discussions within the *palomilla.* They also learn a rich variety of dirty jokes. The game of verbal dueling is played in the *palomilla* where members gain practice and skill.

The *palomilla* members seek adventures as a group. The adventure may be as innocent as taking in a movie together or attending a community dance. Or it may be a boy's first introduction to sex on a date arranged by other members of the *palomilla.* The group gives a fiesta when one of its members marries and participates as a unit in the funeral of a deceased member. The burial of a member may be preceded or followed by an all night drinking party where the virtues of the dead member are extolled.

Palomillas are respected institutions that are not to be confused with the *pachuco* gangs found in large cities of the United States. These gangs develop distinctive modes of dress and speech and either play at the fringes of the law or openly violate it. *Pachucos* are characteristically tattooed with distinctive designs such as a crucifix on the hand. The true *pachuco* gang is an in-group seeking identity and community through revolt against society.

Pachuco gangs are exceedingly rare in Hidalgo County although various manifestations of *pachuco* culture, known as *pachuquismo,* are appearing. Some young men wear the distinctive "duck-tail" haircut and tapered trousers of the *pachuco.* While the tattoo is rare, inked designs on the hand are not uncommon. *Palomillas* that adopt *pachuco* traits are regarded as aberrant and threatening by the Mexican-American community. The symbols of *pachuquismo* are not tolerated in the public schools. A boy who comes to the Mecca school looking like a *pachuco* is sent to the teacher in charge of handling *pachuquismo.* If the boy has a crucifix, a spider, or any other design inked on his hand, it is washed off. Removable symbols of *pachuco* dress, such as the extra-long key chain, are confiscated. The boy is then given money for a haircut and is not allowed back on the school grounds until his duck tail and sideburns have been removed.

Ordinary *palomillas* may occasionally experiment with marijuana but the *pachuco* gangs smoke it regularly. The true *pachucos* sometimes engage in theft and violence. A drunken gang may set out "to show the town." They walk the streets shouting and burlesquing other pedestrians. They may grab another youth disliked by a gang member and beat him. Stabbings and mutilations sometimes occur. These groups are of special concern to the community and they require extra policing.

Pachuquismo is held in check in Hidalgo County primarily by the Mexican-American community. Many cafe owners refuse to serve youths wearing *pachuco* symbols and few hesitate to call the police in the event of unruly behavior. In traditional families, fathers forbid their sons to dress like *pachucos* and mete out severe punishment for disobedience. A *pachuco* knows he will never be allowed near the daughter of a respectable family.

Regardless of whether the *palomilla* is an ordinary one or one that has adopted elements of *pachuquismo,* the main interest is girls. A typical pastime is cruising around in a car and admiring the girls. Every *palomilla* knows of several girls from "scandalous" families who can be dated and seduced. The "easiest marks" are said to be Anglos and anglicized Latin girls. Bragging about seductions provides a popular conversational theme on trips to the north and to neighboring cities. There is little doubt, however, that sex is talked about more than it is experienced. As Timo put it, "If I had had one-tenth of the girls I claimed I had seduced when I was a youth, I'd have been a wonder."

When the time comes for a man to marry, he does not want a girl of the type he has been carnally pursuing. He wants a wife from a family that has protected her chastity and trained her for her wifely duties. "When I'm out for sex," said Felix, "I'm thinking of my own pleasure. When I marry, I'm thinking of the family I represent."

Courtship and Marriage

In the past, it was common for the parents to pick out a suitable girl for their son to marry and then consult him about the matter. Today, the son is more likely to request his parents' consent to marry the girl of his choice. If there is reason to suspect that the parents may not consent to the proposed match, the young couple may politely hint at the possibility of elopement. This hint is often sufficient to elicit the consent of the parents even though they may have some reservations about the marriage.

Formal courtship begins when the boy asks the girl's parents for permission to call on her. If permission is granted, he visits her regularly in her home but never when she is alone. Although kissing is not tolerated by the parents, the young couple may try to sneak an occasional embrace. After obtaining his parents' approval of his marriage plans, the boy may secretly propose to the girl. If she says "yes," a formal proposal is made to her parents.

Today the boy may make a direct proposal to the girl's parents or follow the older custom of making the arrangements through a go-between (*portador*) whose services are secured by his parents. A proper *portador* is a respected member of the community who may be an older woman of good family or a man of good reputation. The *portador* makes the proposal to the girl's parents and they take the matter under consideration for a period of at least two weeks in order to discuss it with their daughter. A polite refusal delivered to the *portador* carries no offense to the boy's family. The *portador* who brings back an acceptance is rewarded with a handsome gift.

Fear of parental refusal to grant permission for marriage is resulting in an increasing number of elopements. Although both sets of parents may express horror at such a marriage, the young couple is often welcomed back. The parents of the bride may even be secretly pleased by the elopement for they are then spared the expense of a wedding ceremony and celebration. Frequently, however, the eloping couple who have been married in a civil ceremony are later remarried in the church at the request of their parents. It is considered improper to consummate a marriage before the church ceremony.

Despite the increase in elopements, most marriages are still performed in the church and followed by a large party. The lavishness of the celebration differs according to class. Lower-class marriages are customarily celebrated with an outdoor barbecue and beer party. Wedding celebrations among the elite sometimes fill the ballrooms of the largest hotels where champagne and imported French delicacies are served in addition to a towering wedding cake. Regardless of these differences, the symbolism is the same. By uniting their children in marriage, the two families have become *compadres* to each other. It is a relationship that endures as long as the marriage.

Mexican-American marriages are usually enduring. The involvement of two entire families behind the marriage bond creates relationships that are difficult to terminate. Moreover, vows taken in the church are held sacred and divorce is regarded as sinful. A wife also knows that divorce will give her a reputation of being a woman of easy virtue regardless of her behavior.

If possible, the newly married couple establish their own home. It is regarded as a kind gesture for the husband to choose a house near the home of the bride's parents. Because the bride is taking on a new familial identification, she finds it comforting to be near her own kin. The husband is also anxious to get as far away as possible from the authority of his father.

The new household follows the patterns of the parents' homes in establishing the husband's authority and the wife's submissiveness. It is a refuge from a hostile world and visiting by unrelated persons is discouraged. Except in anglicized Latin homes, the unrelated visitor is suspect and the male visitor may be a threat to the wife's purity. The home must be kept honorable and secure as a healthy environment for the expected children.

7

Religion

Interpretations of Catholicism

THE MAJORITY OF MEXICAN-AMERICANS are Catholics but their interpretations of Catholicism vary with class and education. The Catholicism of the conservative elite is orthodox and sophisticated. The lower class and a large part of the middle class hold to Spanish-Indian beliefs derived from Mexican folk Catholicism. Such beliefs are the despair of the priests. Sermons delivered in the Magic Valley urge the Latin population to abandon their "superstitions" and accept church dogma. The Mexican-Americans listen politely to these sermons and ignore them.

After one sermon, a Mexican-American was asked what he thought of it. He replied:

> These priests are good and educated men and we must respect them. But they do not understand everything. Their learning comes from books. Any man can become a priest. It is not the best life and some undertake it as a form of penance. It is almost a sin for an only son to enter the priesthood for who will father children for the family? Some priests have children despite their vows but these kids can't bear the family name. That would be a scandal. Even those priests who are very learned can say only what they are told. When a priest says that curers are not to be trusted, ask yourself why he says it. He says it because that is what he has read in the books he has been told to read. But take *Doña* Toribia, the curer. Where does she get her wisdom? Straight from God Himself. She can talk with God so there is no need for her to read the inaccuracies of men's words. Therefore, she knows God's will better than the priest. When one wants help from God, one should go to someone who knows Him. The priest's duty is to say mass. He runs the machinery of the church. He does not see into the trouble of one's soul.

Latin women have a higher regard for priests and a better record of attendance at mass. The mother goes to mass, accompanied by her youngsters, at least once a week. Daughters continue to attend church regularly throughout their lives but boys go less and less regularly after the age of thirteen. Irregular attendance is common among adult males. A Mexican-American father explained:

> I go to church on Easter and Christmas. Sometimes I also go on my saint's day. But what's the advantage of going more often? My wife goes for me and she sees that the kids learn what they should about the church. God is everywhere. You don't have to go to church to see Him. Besides that, I'm tired and like to take it easy on Sunday. My wife can go to mass every day if she wants to. I'll go occasionally to pay my respect to the Lord and let people know I'm a Christian.

Male attendance at church seems to increase with vertical social mobility. A middle-class male gave the reasons for his habit of regular attendance, "I've got a good little business and it is important for me to be respected in the town. Some people lie and say I'm not always fair. I go to church regularly so God will help me put down this gossip. Who could conceive of my going to church on Sunday and cheating somebody on Monday"? A member of the elite gave another explanation for his faithful presence at mass, "These Protestants are all over the place building churches and seducing people from the Faith. People look up to me and I must set an example. With position, I must accept responsibility."

Religion is physically visible in the home at the family altar. The elaborateness of this shrine varies with the wealth and devotion of the family. A typical altar in a lower-class home consists of a table laden with holy images, photographs of deceased relatives, flowers, candles, and an incense burner. In front of one image are leaves of blessed palm and a vial of holy water. Pictures of saints decorate the wall behind the altar. The home of an elite family may house a richly decorated altar in a chapel complete with benches for the worshippers.

Attitudes toward the images range from idolatry to mere appreciation of their beauty. A wife from a lower-class family regarded her image of the Virgin as distinctive and separate from all other images. When it was accidentally broken beyond repair, she suffered agony because her "protector" had been destroyed. A woman of the middle class prays before a statue of the Virgin, "merely because it helps me to visualize her beauty more clearly." She added that the spirit of the Virgin is all around us. A wealthy Latin gentleman prizes an image of St. Francis in his home because it was carved in the seventeenth century.

Devotion to the Saints

Some saints have universal appeal among the Mexican-Americans who call on them for help in a broad range of situations. Other saints are said to have specialized powers in ensuring the success of particular activities. The

Virgin of Guadalupe is widely venerated in Texas but the Mexican-Americans seem to lack the close personal attachment to her that is felt in Mexico. An illiterate Latin said, "The Virgin of Guadalupe is very beautiful and she loves mankind but she lives in Mexico. Her people there keep her busy with their many sins. I do not think she has much time for the Texans. She is so far away."

The Virgin of San Juan is closer to the Mexican-Americans. Her principal shrine is at San Juan de los Lagos in Jalisco, Mexico. The Oblate Brothers dedicated another church to her at San Juan, Texas in 1954. She is a popular patron saint of the Mexican-American family and her image often occupies a prominent position on the home altar.

St. Christopher, the patron saint of travelers, protects the migratory workers. Old Mrs. Ramirez always keeps a candle burning before his image when her son and grandsons go north to harvest crops. She gave each of them a St. Christopher medal to wear while they are traveling. Once they had driven fifty miles from home before discovering that the eldest grandson had forgotten his medal. They returned for it. The father said, "It was probably silly. How can a small piece of silver protect anybody? But it is better to be safe. When you are wearing his medal, St. Christopher can see your trust in him more easily than if he has to reach into your heart. Yes, it is better to be safe."

St. Martin the Horseman (*San Martín Caballero*) is revered particularly by the middle class because he brings success in business. Latin stores often display a small image of St. Martin with an offering of water and grass for his horse. These offerings are considered more important than burning a candle to the saint. Like other saints, St. Martin is believed to be capable of anger as well as love. Mrs. Rivera has been losing faith in St. Martin's ability to attract business for her small store but she does not want to alienate the saint. A friend who visited the store noticed that the glass in front of the image had no water and the wilted grass had turned brown. The visitor commented on this neglect. Mrs. Rivera explained that she had discovered a more efficient means of achieving success in business. A curer had shown her a new technique of bathing herself in water which had been mixed with crushed rose petals on the previous day. Mrs. Rivera added confidentially that she also put in some eau de cologne. She said her business had prospered since she began the baths but "St. Martin is going to be mad at me unless I dust him and feed his horse." Mrs. Rivera fears she will lose all she had gained in her business if St. Martin gets angry.

Images used to be punished in an attempt to coerce the saints to fulfill their obligations but this custom is dying out. Graciela remembers the time when St. Isador *(San Isidro Labrador)* was tormented until he brought rain. Her grandfather's farm was dry and brown from drought. Appeals to the saint went unanswered. Thinking that the saint failed to comprehend the gravity of the situation, the grandfather took the image on a tour to view the desolation of the land. When there was no rain several days later, the image was left to bake in the sun. "Soon it became too uncomfortable for him," Graciela related, "and he convinced God to send the rain. We took San Isidro back indoors and gave him candles as a thanks offering to avert his anger."

Today blessings from saints are most commonly obtained through a contract. In case of serious illness or other disaster, the Mexican-American may promise the saint an offering of candles or a pilgrimage to his shrine in return for supernatural aid. This approach is regarded as eminently rational for it is assumed that the saints keep their human personalities and weaknesses when they ascend to heaven.

An old woman crippled by arthritis asked the Virgin of San Juan to free her son from prison. In return, she promised to walk from her home to the church of the Virgin in San Juan, Texas. When the son was freed a few years ago, the mother began her long and painful trek which was publicized in local newspapers. Her progress was watched with great interest and sympathy. Before reaching the shrine, she appeared to be on the verge of collapse but kept on going because it is considered a horrible sin to break a vow. Divine punishment descends on vow breakers in the form of death or disaster. Friends sought help for the old lady from a priest who walked with her until he was able to convince her that he could give her dispensation from the vow. She finished her pilgrimage by automobile.

Pilgrimages to a host of shrines may be undertaken as a simple act of devotion or as an obligation to fulfill a vow. The further the shrine, the greater the merit of the pilgrimage. Walking to a shrine is more commendable than riding. Very devout individuals complete a final portion of the pilgrimage on their knees. Pilgrimage centers in Mexico impart the greatest blessing to the Mexican-American. A pilgrimage to the Basilica of the Virgin of Guadalupe in Mexico City is usually performed as an act of great devotion rather than in fulfillment of a vow. Few Mexican-Americans seek help from the Mexican saint who lives so far away. Nearer to the border is the shrine of Our Lady of the Springs (*Nuestra Señora de los Chorritos*) south of Linares.

Some Texas shrines are held in reverence. Besides the church of San Juan, Texas, there is the shrine of the Infant Christ (*Santo Niño*) in San Antonio. Other pilgrimage centers in Texas lack the blessing of the Catholic Church. One of these centers is the temple of the miraculous Virgin of Tres Cheques. An old woman who had made a pilgrimage to the temple related the story of its origin:

> An old couple used to live in a little house on the spot where the shrine now stands. One night the old woman saw a light and followed it until she discovered that it came from a stone. She bravely lifted the stone and found an image of the Virgin impressed on it. She took the stone home and kept it. When her son went to the war she prayed to the Virgin of the stone every day that he would return alive. And her prayer was answered. This miracle brought many people from all stations in life to worship here. Both Anglos and Latins came to pray that their sons would return from the war. Many left offerings so that a chapel could be built for the miraculous Virgin. The

> miracles continued. When a *tortilla* was rubbed over the stone one time, an image of the Virgin appeared on it too. Since the war, few people go there. Now they go to see the Virgin of San Juan, Texas. But we should not forget the Virgin of Tres Cheques. Her shrine is a holy and blessed place.

The most famous of the unconsecrated shrines in Texas is that of Don Pedro Jaramillo. During his lifetime, Don Pedrito gained wide renown as a curer. Anglos as well as Latins sought his help. So great is his reputation today that Mexican-Americans have begun to speak of him as San (saint) Pedrito. His shrine in Falfurrias is visited annually by throngs of people seeking his supernatural aid or giving thanks for past favors. Signed petitions for aid and expressions of gratitude are left in the shrine with offerings of candles and flowers.

People appeal to the spirit of Don Pedrito for help in finding work, curing illness, passing school courses, paying bills, and avoiding deportation. Families pray to him for peace and tranquility in the home. Wives ask him to help their husbands quit drinking. Young couples thank him for the birth of healthy babies.

Protestant Proselytism

Reliance on saints and pseudo saints is attacked by Protestant groups that are engaged in missionary activity among the Mexican-Americans of the lower Rio Grande Valley. The Catholics in Latin folk society are tolerant of those who choose to become Protestants but they resent Protestant proselytizing. A Latin Catholic said:

> It is alright to be a Protestant. I don't care what anyone believes as long as he doesn't try to make me swallow his beliefs. That's the trouble. These Protestants do. Some of them even crash into a man's house. I am polite and I let them in and then they set up a phonograph and I have to listen to their lousy records. Then in my own house they attack my faith. They see no truth but their truth and so they insult me. If they had any manners and respect for others, I'd say let them be. But they don't and the next one that comes around is not going to be let in to defile my home.

Some Catholics feel so strongly about door-to-door proselytizing that their homes bear signs reading, "This is a Catholic home. Protestants are not welcomed." Other signs amend the last sentence to read, "Protestants and other salesmen are not welcomed."

The in-fighting among Protestant sects that are competing for Latin converts often amuses the Catholics. A Mexican-American Catholic said: "The only real difference between them and us is that we honor the saints. God is God wherever He is but each Protestant church seems to think He is someone else."

Although most Latin Catholics object only to the intolerance and missionary zeal of the Protestants, a few conservative members of the Latin community see a deeper threat. An old gentleman said:

> Our people have always worshipped God in our own way. Let the Protestants say what they will, our souls will be saved by Catholicism as easily as theirs will be by Protestantism. The way they see God is not what bothers me. It's the way they act. The Protestant way is the Anglo way. Have you ever watched them? Their kids speak out as if they were wise men and even contradict their elders. The Protestants have no respect even in worship. Those alleluias shout and stamp in church as though they were drunk. It's not dignified and it's a poor way to address the Lord. This may be the Anglo way. It's not our way and it never had been.

Some Protestant preachers openly attack Mexican-American loyalty to their religious tradition. A Protestant minister proclaimed that "our way is the way to Progress." A woman missionary also emphasized the value of change, "The Catholics are Catholics because their fathers were. If we change our mode of eating, dressing, and curing the sick, why shouldn't we also change our religious beliefs for the better?"

The differences between Protestantism and Catholicism are viewed by one educated Latin Catholic as different concepts of the nature of man, "The Protestants see only saints and sinners. The Catholics, however, have high esteem for the average person who is seen as neither all good nor all bad. I think the Catholic viewpoint is more realistic and more humanistic."

A more practical objection against the hard-shelled denominations is raised by Latin males. These Protestant sects forbid smoking, consumption of intoxicating beverages, and free pursuit of women. A red-blooded Mexican-American expressed his reaction, "They tell us we should abandon these pleasures so that we can obtain our just rewards. Hell, liquor and women are the rewards I want to receive." On the other hand, many Mexican-American women would welcome these sacrifices on the part of their husbands. Not all of them would, however. One Catholic wife said of her Protestant husband who had recently been converted to a hard-shell church, "I used to be married to a man. Now all I've got is an effeminate husband who thinks everybody outside his church is a sinner. I'm sick and tired of his attempts to save me."

Despite the objections to Protestantism raised by the more conservative Mexican-Americans, Protestant churches are gaining converts among the Latin population. Most of the lower-class and lower-middle class Protestants from the Latin community attend churches where Anglos are rarely seen except for the minister. Latin Protestants of the upper-middle and upper classes constitute a small, loyal, and conspicuous minority in the congregation of an Anglo church. A number of reasons are cited for the segregation of the lower-class Latins in separate churches. Their English is said to be so poor that sermons must be given in Spanish. Because most of them are converts, they require special instruction. A third reason was voiced by an Anglo lady, "They don't dress well, you know, and they eat garlic. I think it might cheapen our church if they worshipped there."

Motives for Conversion

Lower-class converts usually choose one of the fundamentalist sects that are actively seeking their membership. Because these converts are frequently poor people, the Catholics say they are seeking economic gain. "They get free coffee and cake parties and free clothes," Ignacio said. "The Protestant minister helps them get jobs and when they get in trouble he is right there to help them. These Protestants are mostly poor people who can't help themselves." Although Protestant missions used to give away free clothing, this practice ceased when it became apparent that Mexican-American pride forbade the acceptance of such gifts. Today, most missions sell used clothing for a token price that even the poorest families can afford to pay. A suit may sell for fifteen or twenty cents. The mere rite of sale removes this service from the realm of charity.

Some converts join for the convenience of attending a Protestant church that provides free transportation or one that is nearby in an area where the Catholic Church is far away. "The Protestants make it easy to worship in a house of God," a Latin convert said. "I don't think He cares what we call ourselves as long as we go to church and obey His laws."

Latin converts from the middle class choose churches that carry more social prestige in Anglo society. These converts are less prone to "spread the gospel" than lower-class converts. Consequently, they are tolerated and often respected by Mexican-American Catholics.

Protestantism holds the greatest appeal for those members of the Latin middle class who are seeking closer identification with the Anglo way of life. Varying degrees of anglicization are sought by means ranging from the adoption of Anglo customs to an attempt at complete culture transfer. The Mexican-American who denies his own cultural heritage to adopt the Anglo way of life is contemptuously labeled an *inglesado* or *agringado* by more conservative Latins. The *inglesado* typically prizes the Anglo value of individual economic advancement above all other values. He regards the value system of *La Raza* as a handicap to self-development in the world of economic competition. By turning his back on *La Raza,* he hopes to be free to better his economic status. His decision may lead him to discard the beliefs of folk Catholicism.

The Protestant ethic supports the Latin convert in his drive for economic advancement. "When I was a Catholic, my priest urged me to fulfill my obligations to God and my family." said Agustín. "Now I am a Protestant and my minister says that I can best serve God by working hard to better myself."

The Mexican-American convert sometimes sees Protestantism as a form of spiritual and intellectual enlightenment that will rescue him from the darkness of idolatry. "We do not worship man-made images," said Luis. "Praying to the image of a saint is false worship based on ignorance. The saints have no power to answer prayers. Besides, we do not need them to intercede with God. I speak right out to God when I pray now. It is He who answers our prayers—not the saints."

Conversion appears to offer a solution to multiple problems faced by the individual trapped between two cultures. The *inglesado* finds himself in a difficult social and psychological position. His adoption of Anglo goals and mannerisms strains his social relations within the conservative Latin society and rarely ensures full acceptance among the Anglos. Decision-making and self-justification are complicated by reference to both Anglo and Latin values that are incorporated in his mental make-up. As a result of these difficulties, he suffers from extreme anxiety and guilt. Conversion to Protestantism may give him moral support in the struggle for socioeconomic mobility if he adopts the dictum that "God helps those who help themselves." Moreover, the Protestant sects present a simplified value system with a rigid line of demarcation between "right" and "wrong." Full acceptance of Protestant teaching may facilitate decision-making and ease the conscience of the convert. The *inglesado* also hopes that his affiliation with a Protestant church will help him achieve social acceptance in the Anglo community. He sees conversion and the Protestant ethic as keys that will unlock the door to the Anglo world.

Despite the apparent advantages of conversion, the Protestant *inglesado* finds the road to anglicization difficult. The social identity and cultural values that he accepted in childhood cannot be quickly or completely rejected. He is often tormented by feelings of guilt for abandoning his parents and *La Raza.* His adoption of the Anglo-Protestant way of life can also raise serious doubts in his mind about his worth as a real man. In a few cases, extreme psychological stress has resulted in mental breakdown, violence, or both. Such was the case of Juan Gallo.

A Case of Religious Change

Juan grew up in a conservative Catholic family of the lower-middle class. As a child, he was considered an obedient and respectful son. His troubles began in his early teens when he had trouble "holding his own" in a *palomilla.* He took offense too quickly in the verbal dueling games and felt that he was being ridiculed by his companions because of his failures with the girls. Finally, he struck up a close friendship with an anglicized Latin girl in high school but she repulsed his sexual advances. When he proposed marriage, she accepted.

Juan's father forbade the marriage because the girl was an *inglesado* from a Protestant family and she had a reputation of being morally lax. In defiance of his father's authority, Juan ran away from home and married the girl in a Protestant church ceremony attended by her family. Shortly after the marriage, Juan was baptized in his wife's church. He deliberately avoided any attempt at reconciliation with his parents and consciously set out to become an economic success within the framework of Anglo society. He found a job in an Anglo grocery store where his dedication and willingness to work overtime soon earned him a promotion and pay raise.

The young couple spoke English at home and avoided using Spanish whenever possible. They also avoided the Spanish-language movies and the Latin restaurants where Juan's former friends might be encountered. In dress and mannerism, the couple tried to imitate Anglo custom.

Juan made an effort to be a good member of his Protestant church. He became a teetotaler and stayed away from beer parlors. He avoided contact with women other than his wife and condemned male preoccupation with sex in the Mexican-American community. His attempt to give up smoking proved to be too much for his new-found Protestant character but he did stop smoking at home and on the church grounds.

He renounced the symbols of *machismo* not only in public but also in his home. There he helped his wife with the dishes and housework in an attempt to be a good husband by Anglo standards. Such household tasks would never be willingly performed by a "true man" in conservative Latin society. Once Juan suffered acute embarrassment when he opened the door of his house for an unexpected visitor and then realized that he was still wearing a dish towel around his waist like an apron. Juan's anxiety about his *machismo* was heightened by the fact that his wife had failed to conceive a child after two years of marriage.

Nevertheless, Juan buttressed his self-image as a man with success achieved in his job, sports, and civic activities. At the grocery store he progressed to the point where he was being considered for the position of manager and he confidently expected to receive this honor. He starred in an outstanding baseball team sponsored by his church. Some of his church friends persuaded him to join a patriotic men's group working for increased participation of the Mexican-Americans in local politics. Several times, his minister congratulated him on his role as a civic-minded Protestant and an active member of the church.

Juan's new world blew up in one day. When he went to work that day, he learned that an Anglo had been chosen for the position of store manager. The same afternoon, his baseball team suffered its first major defeat of the season. Juan made a series of errors in the game and shouldered full responsibility for the team's defeat. He returned home and told his wife of the disasters. She became furious over his failure to obtain the promotion and accused him of lacking the courage to stand up for his rights "like a man." In silent anger, she served him chicken soup for supper. Juan took this act as an insult implying that he was "chicken." He noticed that the soup contained internal organs used in folk magic to enhance female beauty.

Juan exploded in a violent display of anger. He accused his wife of magically depriving him of his male powers so she would be free to take a lover. When he began beating her, the neighbors heard her screams and called the police. A short time later there was a knock on the door. Juan grabbed his revolver and shouted to his wife that he was going to "fix" her lover. Throwing open the door, he shot the policemen between the legs. Juan was arrested and declared legally insane. He was transferred to a mental institution.

Very few of the Mexican-Americans who attempt cultural transfer suffer the extreme trauma experienced by Juan Gallo. However, similar anxieties and fears of lesser degree afflict most *inglesados.* The tragedy of Juan Gallo can be interpreted from various viewpoints. A psychologist probably would be most interested in the collapse of Juan's self-image as a man. An anthropologist might explain his crisis as the result of value conflicts. A folk Catholic would say that Juan was punished for offending God. A Protestant might think Juan failed to summon up his moral fortitude and God-given strength. Mexican-American folk society sees his suffering as the just desserts of a traitor to *La Raza.* The Anglos may point to him as an example of the unreliability and inadequacy of the Mexican-Americans. Juan himself probably feels today that he was guilty of violating the authority of his father, betraying the sacred love of his mother, and offending God.

8

Sickness and Health

Supernatural Causation

THE MEMBERS of *La Raza* do not divide the natural and the supernatural into separate compartments as the Anglos do. An harmonious relationship between the natural and the supernatural is considered essential to human health and welfare, while disharmony precipitates illness and misfortune.

Views vary on the extent of supernatural causation. The lower class sees the natural and the supernatural blended into one functional totality. Therefore, the members of this class rely heavily on supernatural techniques in dealing with illness and other problems. Conservative members of the middle class have a more secular orientation toward the problems of daily life but still perceive a supernatural power pervading the universe. The conservative elite preserves a religious philosophy but scorns the superstitions of the lower class. The anglicized upper class tends to adopt popular scientific concepts of natural order and causation. Through education and other contacts with the Anglo world, the younger generation of all classes has become increasingly skeptical of supernatural beliefs derived from Mexican folk medicine.

The lower-class Latin never challenges or ridicules the subjective beliefs of others but he is well aware that the Anglos ridicule most of his ideas concerning supernaturalism. Consequently, he is reluctant to discuss his supernatural beliefs and practices with Anglos or anglicized Latins. The middle-class Latin may hesitate to admit belief in folk medicine even among his fellow Latins for they might think him unscientific.

Many Mexican-Americans are caught in the conflict between the scientific theories of modern medicine and the supernatural theories of folk medicine. In the event of illness, it is considered prudent to take every possible precaution including both natural and supernatural approaches. Even the sophisticated Latin sometimes relies on folk medicine although he may be ashamed to admit it to the outside world.

Raymond, a Latin member of the upper-middle class, pointed out the ambivalence of his fathers views on folk medicine:

> Dad always says we should forget this nonsense that the *curanderos* (folk curers) tell us about witchcraft and the evil eye. At home, he makes jokes about the *curanderos* and about my aunt who runs to them whenever she gets sick. But then he got boils on his head and they were still there after he had been treated by a doctor for a week. My mother kept urging him to see a *curandero* but he just laughed at her. Later, my cousin told me that he actually went to see one. He sneaked in the back door so no one would see him and he didn't even tell us.

Raymond added, "I don't believe in these quacks myself. They just prey on the superstitions of the poor. But you know, it's a funny thing. Right after Dad saw the *curandero,* his boils went away. It was kind of miraculous."

A qualified acceptance of such '"miracles" penetrates the ranks of the Latin upper class, which openly denounces Mexican superstitions. A Mexican-American lawyer offered this commentary on *curanderismo:*

> Of course, its all nonsense but curious things do happen. My sister was unable to bear children despite her visits to numerous doctors. She finally went to see a *curandero* in Monterey. I don't know what all went on there but I'm sure there was a lot of praying and many herbs went down her throat. Less than a year later she had a baby. Some of those Indian herbs are alright. Don't forget that most of our medicines are derived from them. And the *curandero* gave my sister faith that she could bear children. Maybe it had nothing to do with her treatment by the *curandero.* But you can't deny she had the baby.

Faith in folk medicine is strongest among members of the lower class who see supernatural forces in every phase of life from conception to death. A well-known midwife explained the process of conceiving a new life, "It is a marvelous and divine thing. The power of life in man unites with that of woman in her womb. It happens in a sacred instant while God presides over the event. From that moment on, the new being develops in the mother's womb by the will of God."

A strong bond is said to exist between a newly-conceived baby and the father. Sometimes this bond is so powerful that the father experiences symptoms associated with pregnancy. Susana first learned that she was pregnant when her husband developed morning nausea.

Pregnancy and Childbirth

Pregnancy is considered to be a dangerous period for the unborn child. It is believed that emotional and physical upsets of the pregnant woman may affect the health and development of the fetus. Strange and powerful forces accompanying certain natural phenomena can deform the infant in the womb. The reflections of a lunar eclipse and the light of a full moon are regarded as particularly dangerous. Some Latin women wear a key suspended by a string belt over the abdomen in order to protect the embryonic child against deformity.

An expectant mother must remain in harmony with the universe throughout pregnancy. If she is exposed to any unusual or upsetting experience, she must take precautionary measures to maintain this harmonious relationship. "A healthy and serene mother will bring a healthy child into the world," a midwife said. "It is a perfectly normal thing to bear a child. I don't know why pregnant Anglo women run to a doctor as if they were ill. Treating a pregnant woman like an invalid can only upset the little life within her. The doctors should not interfere with the way God intended children to develop within their mothers' wombs."

Despite the advice of the midwives, modern medical care during pregnancy and childbirth is becoming the norm in the Magic Valley. Still, some of the old-fashioned women believe that home births are better for the child than the antiseptic and impersonal environment of a hospital delivery room. Tomasa said, "The doctors can make it easier for you to expel the child from your womb but I don't believe that it is right for a baby to be born in a hospital. The child should enter the world in the home where he will be raised and surrounded by love."

Home births usually take place with the assistance of midwives whose practical ministrations are accompanied by prayers and rites intended to protect the life of the mother and child. "As soon as I deliver a baby, I bless the child to remind him that his safe delivery came about because of God's loving care," a Latin midwife said. "I may assist the baby's passage but only God is responsible for its healthy delivery. I am but a servant of God."

A good midwife continues to take an interest in the children she has delivered as long as they live. Incarnacion, a midwife, affectionately greets someone she has delivered and refers to him as "one of my dear children." When "her children" misbehave, their mothers often bring them to Incarnacion for admonishment and advice on proper behavior. "They listen to me and respect what I tell them," she said. "This is because I can say to them, 'Why I gave you your first spanking even before your mother touched you'. I saw these children into the world and it is my duty to see that they remain good and healthy."

Health and well-being after birth continue to depend on the maintenance of a God-given balance in life. Any disruption of the balanced relationship between parts of the body, between the individual and society, or between human beings and supernatural beings can produce illness and distress.

Theory of Balanced Relationships

Many *curanderos* and some of the recent migrants from Mexico believe that a healthy body must maintain an even balance of "hot" and "cold" qualities associated with the four humors: blood, phlegm, choler (the yellow bile of anger), and melancholia (the black bile of depression). This physiological theory is a legacy from colonial Mexico where the Spaniards introduced the system of Hippocratic medicine in the sixteenth century. Hippocratic medicine still flourishes in rural Mexico but is dying out among the Latins in south Texas.

Since a healthy body is conceived as being a temperate blend of "hot" and "cold" components, illness is seen as an imbalance resulting in either a hot or cold condition. A hot ailment is treated by cold medications and foods while the reverse treatment is recommended for cold diseases. The classification of hot or cold refers to the effect of the food or medication on the human body. Chile and ice are classified as hot because they burn the mouth. Watermelon is cold because it is full of water, which cools the mouth.

Excessive consumption of either hot or cold foods is said to produce a bodily imbalance resulting in illness. Sickness is also caused by strong emotions such as anger or grief, which upset the balance of the humors and produce abnormal temperatures. Some Mexican-Americans believe that certain periods of life tend to induce extremes of body temperature, which must be offset by dietary precautions. Adolescence is said to be a hot period because of accelerated sexual drives. Therefore, teen-agers should be fed cold foods to prevent illness and control their passions. Old age is a cold period because of the ebbing of the life force. Consequently, the aged should eat an abundance of hot foods.

Certain individuals are said to be subject to a hot or cold extreme in body temperature throughout life. As a *curandera* explained, "The blood of some people is too hot and they are always sweating. Others have cold blood and they cannot sweat even on hot days. If such people are wise, they try to correct their condition by eating the appropriate hot or cold foods. Otherwise, they suffer from frequent illness."

Other imbalances within the body cause illness. The dislocation of a bone or shifting of an organ results in the malfunctioning of the body as a whole. Foreign objects or evil forces entering the body can cause illness as can the loss of a vital part of the body or the spirit. Immoral behavior that disrupts the harmony between the individual and his social or spiritual environment can bring on sickness. Strife in interpersonal relations may cause an antagonist to employ the forces of evil to bewitch his enemy.

Classification of Disease

Mexican-American folk medicine classifies disease mainly according to cause rather than symptoms. The primary classification of disease distinguishes two major categories: 1) the so-called "good" or "natural" illnesses, which come from violating the balance of the natural world controlled by God; and 2) bewitchments sent by human adversaries utilizing evil Satanic forces. A natural illness is corrected by restoring the particular balance that was disrupted.

Bewitchment is cured by countermagic or by removing the immediate source of harm.

A different classification of disease is used by the more anglicized Latins who are abandoning some tenets of folk medicine. Some of them use the term "natural diseases" for illness resulting from natural phenomena such as infection or accident. In the category of supernatural illnesses, they lump together diseases sent by God and the Devil. The extent of belief in supernatural diseases depends on the degree of anglicization. The concept of illness as punishment from God falls in the realm of ideas that are most resistant to change. Many of the conservative elite firmly believe in punitive disease. The anglicized upper class openly denounces belief in all supernatural ailments.

According to the theories of folk medicine, natural disease may result from either wilful or unconscious disruption of the balance of God's world. Afflictions that result from taking deliberate risks are called *enfermedades buscadas* (sought-for illnesses). This term is most commonly used in reference to sexual diseases connected with prostitution. It may also be used to designate the results of stupid behavior involving great risk. Thus, it was said that Juan sought out his broken leg by racing his old car at full throttle while he was drinking.

The classification of natural diseases distinguishes illnesses recognized by modern medicine from those that are unique to folk medicine. The first category includes such diseases as colds, influenza, pneumonia, whooping cough, measles, and appendicitis. Anglicized Latins and the elite accept the scientific etiology of these diseases and rely on modern medicine for treatment although they do not always discount the possibility that God may have sent the germs that caused an illness. The members of Mexican-American folk society frequently seek modern medical treatment for contagious and organic diseases but they do not fully accept the scientific explanation of disease causation.

Much of the opposition to modern medicine stems from the rejection of the germ theory of disease. Mexican-Americans of the lower class are aware of the germ concept but many of them refuse to recognize the actual existence of microbes. Germs are thought of as mythical little animals called *animalitos.* Because these creatures cannot be seen by the naked eye, they are often dismissed as an invention dreamed up by Anglo doctors to dupe the people. The majority of uneducated Mexican-Americans have never looked through a microscope. Their view of microscopic life comes from cartoons shown in TV advertisements and public health clinics. They do not find this evidence very convincing.

"When they show me a live, moving germ that I can see and touch, then I'll believe," said old Joaquin. "Those stupid TV pictures of little animals that look like fly specks or Mickey Mice mean nothing."

A public health nurse who makes regular home visits scolded Rosa for allowing her new baby to drink from a bottle after flies had touched the nipple. "You must see that the nipple is crawling with germs," the Anglo nurse said. After the nurse departed, Rosa carefully examined the nipple and then gave the bottle back to her baby. "There is nothing on it at all," she commented to her mother who was visiting at the time. "That nurse must have spots on her glasses."

Despite such incredulity, the germ theory of disease is slowly gaining acceptance among the Mexican-Americans. Public health education has promoted some change of belief. More important is the classroom education of children. Many parents refuse to accept the ideas their children bring home from school but experimentation with patent medicines has led them to believe in the possible existence of germs. When such medicines bring relief, some Mexican-Americans accept advertising claims that the efficiency of the medication is due to its power to kill germs. "When I have a sore throat, I buy this gargle and it always makes my throat feel better," Valentin explained. "Maybe it really is like it says on the label that the hurt comes from germs biting me." A major incentive for the acceptance of the germ theory is the fact that a number of respected *curanderos* attribute certain diseases to the little animals and prescribe scientific medications along with prayers.

Doña Magdalena, an outstanding *curandera,* admits that germs cause many diseases but warns that medicine alone rarely effects a cure, "It is true that an innocent person may sometimes contract a disease that can be cured by medication, but more often germs are the tools of God. They may be sent to punish a sin. Then no amount of medicine will cure the ailment. First, one must makes his peace with God. Then the medicine will work but only then." Cancer is nearly always described as a punishment from God. The fact that Anglo doctors can rarely cure cancer is cited as proof that mere medication does not enable man to thwart the will of God.

Symptomatic treatment for diseases of all categories utilizes Anglo patent medicines administered at home. Aspirin is taken for headache, fever, and generalized pain. Ground aspirin mixed with lard may be rubbed over the patient's body to reduce fever. Commercial gargles are used for sore throat. Vicks Vaporub and Mentholatum are applied externally for chest congestion and sore throat. Other home remedies are far removed from the Anglo medicine cabinet. A persistent cough may be treated by smoking a cigarette made of salvia, an herb belonging to the sage family. The herb must be dried on a griddle, ground, and wrapped in cigarette paper or newspaper. A popular remedy for stomach cramps is an herb tea made of *istafiate* (*Artemisia Mexicana*).

Treatment of symptoms alone is considered useless. The cause of the illness must be removed if the patient is to be restored to health. Despite growing reliance on physicians for treatment of those diseases recognized both by folk medicine and scientific medicine, Mexican-Americans believe that other folk diseases can be cured only by folk medicine. Prominent among the ailments peculiar to folk medicine are bewitchment, evil eye, fright, and fallen fontanel. These folk diseases are completely alien to medical science that labels them as superstitions. Medical denial of the existence of such diseases is taken as evidence of the limited knowledge of physicians.

Folk diseases unrecognized by modern medicine are not referred to physicians unless there is doubt about the diagnosis or suspicion of complications amenable to supplementary scientific treatment. Mild sickness is treated at home by the mother, the grandmother, or another elderly female relative who has special knowledge of folk medicine. Severe illness is referred to *curanderos*

In either case, certain basic procedures of folk curing are followed to reestablish the internal and external balance of the patient.

One of the most common treatments is the cleansing performed by brushing the patient's body with branches of curing herbs or an unbroken egg in order to draw the disease out of the body into the externally applied object. Poultices also are used to absorb the illness. External treatment is accompanied by internal use of herb teas to combat the illness and soothe the patient. Massage and manual pressure are used to rearrange parts of the body that have gotten out of place. Bodily aches are sometimes treated by massaging the muscles with snake oil purchased in the herb stores. All techniques of folk curing are accompanied by prayers and appeals to God and the saints for help.

Childhood Diseases

Many of the unique folk diseases occur during the precarious period of childhood when the youngster lacks physical and spiritual adjustment to life. The delicate balance of the child is easily upset during infancy. Special attention is paid to the infant's head because the bones are not yet set. Some mothers believe an infant should wear a tight cap to fix the bones and the shape of the head. It is considered important to avoid jarring the baby since a fall or jolt can dislodge the fontanel causing it to collapse. The balance of the fontanel and the palate are said to be correlated so that the imbalance of one affects the other. Mothers are careful not to abruptly pull a nipple from the mouth of a sucking infant because this action could pull down the palate and the fontanel. The ailment known as fallen fontanel is recognized by symptoms such as excessive crying, insomnia, digestive upsets, and loss of appetite. The baby may or may not be feverish. A positive diagnosis can be made by feeling the top of the baby's head to detect the unusual depression characteristic of fallen fontanel.

The mother or grandmother of the sick child administers the home cure for fallen fontanel. The most common procedure is for the adult to insert both thumbs into the infant's mouth and push gently upward on the palate. The baby is usually cradled in the arms of a female relative during the treatment. Sometimes, the baby is held upside down by his ankles on the theory that the force of gravity helps push the fontanel back into place. An alternate treatment applies suction rather than upward pressure. The adult may place his open mouth over the baby's fontanel and gently suck. Another technique based on the suction theory consists of covering the fontanel with a poultice of herbs mixed with a beaten raw egg. Water may be used as the drawing power to pull the fontanel up into place. In this case, the water can be dipped over the baby's bowed head or applied to a cloth placed on top of the fontanel.

Although fallen fontanel is probably the most common ailment of infancy in the folk community, there are other childhood afflictions treated by folk medicine. The infant may suffer from an emotional disturbance and upset stomach if his mother becomes pregnant again before he is weaned. "The baby thinks his new brother in his mother's womb is stealing his milk," Maria said. "The little creature within the mother may turn the milk sour or stop its flow to prevent the other child from emptying the mother's breasts. The ailing baby cries in anger and may lose his sucking ability when he is afflicted with this illness known as *chipil.* The best remedies are extra attention, love, and soothing herb teas. This ailment is becoming rare as bottle feeding becomes more and more popular.

The sickness called *sereno* (evening dew) causes pus formation in the corners of the baby's eyes or makes them run. The infant's clothing must be smoked over an herb fire made of rosemary in order to warm the sick child and draw out the disease.

Evil air may enter the body of a child or an adult producing aches in the particular area where it lodges. This Mexican concept of evil air sickness is being replaced by the Anglo theory of a cold caused by a draft. In any case, it is considered wise to protect a child from cold winds and night air.

Children suffer from a form of indigestion known as *empacho,* which may afflict adults. Undigested food is said to form a ball on the wall of the stomach or intestine causing pain around the navel. Empacho is cured by removing the ball of foodstuff through the use of purgative herbs and massage. The treatment for children involves rubbing the stomach and back with oil in a downward manipulation designed to help the food pass out of the body. The skin on the lower part of the back is pinched and pulled at the sides in order to straighten out twisted muscles blocking passage of the food. The dried herb called *hoja sen* (*Cassia diphylla, Legumunosae*) is mixed with cotton thread, burned to ashes, and mixed with milk that is fed to the child to break up the ball of food. After the child has passed the food, his upset stomach is soothed by an infusion of *istafiate* boiled with milk. Because the treatment makes the child weak, he must be kept warm afterward.

Several explanations are given for the cause of empacho. The members of folk society say it can be caused by a severe emotional experience or by eating too many heavy foods such as bananas, rice, and potatoes, which get stuck in the stomach. A more anglicized explanation came from a middle-class merchant who said, "Empacho is nothing but pure constipation. It can be cured in twenty minutes by a dose of salts. Of course, the laborers see it as something else. But give them time and education and they will learn."

Some folk diseases are not so easily equated with a scientific diagnosis by the anglicized Latins. The diseases of evil eye, fright, and bewitchment involve supernatural connotations that violate Anglo concepts of disease etiology. Evil-eye sickness is unintentionally inflicted by a person possessing "strong vision." He is born with a strange power in his eyes beyond his control. Because he cannot manipulate this power and may not even be aware of it, the possessor of strong vision is deemed guiltless when he accidentally causes illness.

The force of the evil eye is unconsciously projected by the possessor into any person, animal, or object he admires. Although Mexican-Americans do not say so, the evil eye is, to some extent, a reflection of envy. This force enters people or things not belonging to the viewer who desires or envies them. Children are especially susceptible to evil-eye sickness because they lack the spiritual and physical strength of the adult. The power of the evil eye may also destroy personal property that is admired. One day, Cecilia admired a new vase purchased by her mother-in-law, Felicia. The next day Felicia found a large crack in the vase that she attributed to an unconscious projection of Cecilia's evil eye. Felicia's brother said, "I think the vase got cracked when the kids were horsing around in here last night while the old folks were out. But let Felicia think what she wants. It makes her feel better to think that the vase was admired so much. It also gives her something to gossip about. I don't think she really likes Cecilia."

Unconscious hostility may be expressed in attributing powerful vision to another person even though he is not openly blamed for the damage he causes. Desired avoidance of an individual also may be rationalized on the grounds that the person possesses the evil eye. Mrs. Webster is a kind-hearted and devoted public health nurse whose bustling authoritarianism makes her unwelcome when she visits Latin homes. She is greeted politely but her presence is obviously resented. She is unaware of the fact that she has the reputation of possessing the evil eye and spreading sickness among the Mexican-American children whom she admires. She is the subject of female gossip throughout the Latin community because she behaves improperly and poses a threat to children. "How can we trust her statement that she understands disease and wants to help us?" Juana asked. "She is either stupid or inconsiderate to admire so many kids when she has strong vision and then not even try to prevent the sickness by touching them."

If Mrs. Webster were to caress or rub the head of each child she admires, there would be no cause for complaint. Touching the person or thing admired removes the harmful force of the evil eye. Most conservative Latins take the precaution of touching a child's head after admiring his beauty.

Evil-eye sickness can be easily cured but it produces very serious results if it goes untreated. The symptoms range from simple nervousness to rashes, sores, aches, and pains. The disease is manifested in children by insomnia, trembling, and intensive crying that may or may not be accompanied by fever.

The simplest treatment is to locate the person responsible for the sickness and request him to pat the patient's head or rub his temples. The person possessing strong vision usually complies with this request without taking offense. However, it is often difficult to identify the person who caused the sickness. The most common treatment consists of rubbing the patient's body with an unbroken raw egg to draw out the evil force. After this cleansing ritual, the egg is broken and the liquid contents are poured into a glass of water. The formation of the egg indicates whether the diagnosis of evil-eye sickness was correct and the cure successful. The significance of the egg formation is interpreted in different ways. Some say that if the yolk rises to the center of the glass, it is a sure sign that the evil-eye sickness has been drawn out of the body. Others say that the egg white must form the shape of an eye on the surface of the water to indicate a successful cure. Still others maintain that the egg should look as though it has been cooked for a little while if the treatment has been effective. Sometimes, the glass containing the egg mixture is left under the patient's bed for the night to remove any remaining sickness. The egg and water must be carefully disposed of after the treatment for they are considered infectious. The contents of the glass are usually buried in the yard away from plants that may be withered by the evil-eye force.

John, an anglicized teacher, recalls being treated for evil-eye sickness during childhood in his conservative Latin home:

> I remember those days well. Although I don't believe in the evil eye today, I was often treated for evil-eye sickness and the cure usually worked. Looking back, I think the treatment did two things for me. It demonstrated my family's love for me and it made me feel important. I was always jealous of my older brothers, especially when my father praised them for doing well at things I was too young to try. I also must have resented the love showered on the youngest baby in the family. When I felt left out and neglected as a kid, I'd get awfully upset sometimes. I would cry and sulk and really didn't know why. My mother would notice and say I suffered from the evil eye. Then I was the center of the family and everyone would try to make me comfortable. I felt important when the others watched me being cleaned with an egg. When I was tucked in for the night I was surrounded by love and concern. Those minutes before I dropped off to sleep were full of happiness and security.

Fright Sicknesses

Children suffer from fright sicknesses although they are associated with adulthood more often than is evil-eye sickness. *Curanderos* and some of the older members of *La Raza* distinguish *susto* and *espanto* as two different diseases caused by fright. *Susto* is attributed to natural fright that might occur in a narrow escape from being run over by a truck. *Espanto* is caused by a supernatural occurrence such as an encounter with a ghost. One *curandera* separated the two diseases on the basis of the part afflicted in the sick person, irrespective of the cause of the fright. "*Espanto* occurs when the spirit is frightened," she said. "*Susto* results when the heart is frightened. Both of these things can happen after a terrible experience." The average Mexican-American does not make these fine distinctions. He lumps the two diseases together as one affliction that may be called either *susto* or *espanto* although the first term is preferred.

There is lack of agreement as to how fright affects the human body. Some say that fright either paralyzes the soul or forces it out of the body. The same belief in soul loss is found in the folk cultures of Mexico. Another theory in the Magic Valley presumes that fright sickness is caused by an undefined evil that enters the body and must be removed to effect a cure. A Mexican-American with a high school education gave a different explanation, "Fright is a real disease recognized by doctors who call it by another name. Just because we call it *susto* or *espanto,* the Anglos mock it as superstition. Anyone who has been frightened may become ill. Call it 'shock' or 'nerves' like the Anglos and people will say you are scientific."

Innumerable sources of fright can afflict a person while he is asleep or awake. A *curandero* told Olivia that her sick baby was suffering from fear of his own shadow. Olivia thinks the curer is right because the baby used to lie on his stomach, raise himself up like a seal, and watch his shadow reflected on the floor by an overhead light. Enrique fled in terror from a huge phantom encountered on the way home from a late night in a beer parlor. The next day he was sick with fright. Margarita dreamed constantly of the hell fire and eternal torment that she would endure in the afterworld because of her sinful life as a prostitute. These nerve-wracking nights gave her an extreme case of fright. Pedro escaped to safety after being chased by an enraged bull dog but the aftermath of his experience was fright sickness. Emotional arguments and self pity can cause fright illness.

The symptoms of fright are exhaustion, restlessness, and loss of appetite. The patient loses interest in all activity and often refuses to eat. He may experience pain and develop sores on his body. When these symptoms are observed by the family of the sick person, he is urged to try to remember any frightening experience that might have caused his illness. If he does recall such an experience from the recent past, the diagnosis of fright sickness is confirmed. Some *curanderos* detect fright sickness by taking the patient's pulse. This method of diagnosis was described by a folk curer, "The pulse of an *asustado* or *espantado* is irregular. Most of the time it is weak and slow but then it will run like a frightened thing. Then it slows down again until one thinks it is going to stop."

Referral to a *curandero* is indicated if the fright sickness appears to be serious or fails to respond to home treatment. The services of a *curandero* are considered essential in advanced cases of fright that have developed complications due to lack of treatment. Advanced fright sickness is known as *susto pasado.* The symptoms are prolonged exhaustion and coughing or fits. In the rare cases when a physician is consulted, this illness is often diagnosed as tuberculosis or epilepsy.

There are many techniques for treating fright and more than one may be used. The blessing of a priest is sought in cases thought to be caused by ghosts. A cross may be painted with lime on the patient's bed or cradle. Herb medicines are taken internally in most cases of fright sickness. An infusion of *altamisa,* an herb belonging to the ambrosia genus, may be administered three times daily for nine days. An alternate herb remedy is prepared by boiling the herb anise with three crosses made of red ribbon. A less common treatment consists of feeding the patient water mixed with dirt taken from the center of a crossroad. Internal remedies are commonly accompanied by external brushings with broom straws or branches of the herb called *escobilla* in order to cleanse the patient of the evil within his body.

The most highly regarded cure for fright is performed only by *curanderos.* Doña Juanita described this treatment:

> First, I diagnosis the case by cleaning the patient's body with an egg. When I crack the shell and drop the raw egg into a glass of water, I can tell whether the affliction is fright or another illness. Some of the disease enters the egg and you can see it is fright by the way the egg white curls in the water. Sometimes, I also feel the patient's pulse. An irregular pulse means that he has *latido,* an exhaustion that often comes from fright. To treat the patient, I must remove the fright from his body.
>
> My treatment lasts nine days. You must understand that it is not I, but God, who really cures. I pray constantly and so does my patient. Throughout the treatment, I give the patient purifying and strengthening teas. I sweep his body daily with an herb bundle containing *albahaca* (sweet basil), *poleo* (pennyroyal), and *romero* (rosemary). The most important part of the cure consists of drawing an outline of his body in dirt three times a day. The patient lies on a dirt floor while I use a knife to cut an outline of his body in the ground. When he rises, I take dirt from the lines cut in the ground and mix it with water for him to drink. This I do three times a day for nine days. During each treatment, I say nine Lord's Prayers and nine Hail Marys. On the final day of the cure, the last thing I do is recite the Twelve Truths of the World forward and backward. Then, if it is God's will, the patient is well.

Fright sickness is one of the folk diseases that afflicts only members of *La Raza.* Anglos are considered immune to these diseases. One *cuarandero said:*

> I do not know why God has afflicted only us with evil eye, *empacho,* fallen fontanel, fright, and many other diseases. But God is merciful. He sent us these afflictions but he also taught us how to cure them. No gringo doctor will ever learn how to cure these sicknesses. They come to us and only we understand them. Only we of *La Raza* can cure them. Some of us, like myself, have been blessed by God and through his blessing we have become curers. God sends disease to punish us but he also lets us learn to repent and undo the suffering. His great concern must reflect a very great love for *La Raza.* You punish most the erring children whom you love best. Therefore, it is not strange that the Anglos never suffer these divinely sent afflictions.

9

Witchcraft

Beliefs

Bewitchment is the most dreaded of all folk diseases. Unlike the "good" diseases that are accepted as a natural part of God's world, bewitchment is associated with Satan and evil. The term witchcraft is used in the valley to include black magic as well as Satanic power wielded by the witch. Both forms of witchcraft are regarded as blasphemy. Witches, it is said, surely go to hell.

The "good" or "natural" folk diseases are largely unknown to most of the English-speaking population, so Anglo contempt for Latin superstitions is directed mainly at witchcraft beliefs. Because the Latins want to avoid ridicule, they are reluctant to discuss witchcraft beliefs with strangers or casual acquaintances. If a Mexican-American mentions a case of witchcraft outside of his family circle, he usually refers to it as mere heresay. When the listener registers credulity, the Latin may discuss the bewitchment as a reality. If skepticism is manifested, the speaker dismisses witchcraft as a belief of fools.

Belief in witchcraft remains strong among the adult members of the lower classes and the lower-middle class. Skepticism is widespread in the upper-middle class although witchcraft beliefs are occasionally encountered there. The elite and the anglicized members of the upper class dismiss witchcraft as a belief of the lowly and uneducated people. The younger generation of the lower and middle classes tend to doubt the reality of witchcraft more than the existence of "good diseases," such as fright or *empacho.* Witchcraft is denounced more frequently than other folk disease theories in the press, the schools, and the pulpit.

European Satanic beliefs are combined with the witchcraft beliefs of pre-Conquest Mexico in the folklore of the Magic Valley. It is said that a witch obtains power from Satan enabling him[1] to harm his victims through magical

[1] Although the word "witch" usually refers to a woman, the anthropological literature on Latin America is full of references to both male and female witches. In Mexico and Texas the term "witch" *(brujo)* is applied to male and female practitioners of witchcraft. Most

rites. The witch's powers include the ability to fly and transform himself into animal shapes. Some people say that witches can become invisible and listen in on your conversations. This is another reason why it is unwise to discuss the subject of witchcraft too freely.

Witches are frequently said to take the form of cats. Elsa took to feeding a stray cat that soon came regularly for his plate of scraps. She was fond of the animal. Caring for the cat was a relief from the horrible arguments she had been having with her husband recently. Her marital fights later became so frequent and unpleasant that Elsa sought advice from a *curandera.* The curer divined that the trouble stemmed from a hex placed on the couple by a woman who wanted to steal the affections of Elsa's husband. The curer said the witch would appear near Elsa's house in the form of a cat or an owl to see whether the hex was working. *"Madre Mio de Dios!"* exclaimed Elsa, "I have been feeding a stray cat since our fighting began." "It is the witch," announced the curer. "When you see the cat next," she told Elsa, "pour boiling water on it and the witch will be too pained to continue her evil." Elsa returned home and told her husband the truth about their arguments and the cat. The husband objected that scalding the cat would hold them up to the ridicule of their neighbors but Elsa insisted on carrying out the *curandera's* advice and put a pot of water on to boil. The husband ran to the back yard and hurled rocks at the cat until it fled never to return. Elsa interpreted her husband's action as an indication of his hatred for the woman who had hexed them. After that, Elsa reported that she and her husband had fewer arguments.

A witch may take the form of an owl to fly over the home of her victim. It is said that the correct ritual can force the witch-bird to fall down. One rite consists of saying forty credos and tying a knot in a ribbon at the end of each prayer. In another version, the oration called *The Twelve Truths of the World* is recited forwards and backwards. The witch is then supposed to fall to earth in human form.

Felipe often tells his daughter how he trapped a witch who had hexed his wife shortly after their marriage. While his wife lay ill in bed, Felipe went outside and recited the forty credos as required. Suddenly, there appeared a woman lying on the ground crumpled and moaning as though she had fallen from a great height. Felipe quickly opened his pocket knife to a ninety degree angle and stuck it into the front door to "fix" the witch to the spot and prevent her from doing more evil while she was there. Then Felipe demanded that the witch remove the hex but she refused. "Alright," Felipe responded, "lie there all night in the cold and maybe tomorrow you will be more reasonable." He entered the house and closed the door with the witch-holding knife still in it. Unfortunately, the knife was stolen during the night by a thief who did not notice the witch and she was freed. When Felipe came out in the morning, the witch was gone. He believes that he frightened her enough to make her remove the hex for his wife recovered soon afterward.

---

witches in Texas are said to be females, but Mexican-Americans refer to male witches from Mexico who are hired to hex Texas residents. In this paragraph the word "him" is used in the neuter sense to refer to anyone who practises witchcraft.

A witch can be deprived of his power by removing some of his blood. Rosa tells the story of how she destroyed the witch powers of her daughter-in-law, Angela. After Angela's husband was killed in an automobile accident, the girl moved in with her in-laws because she had no family in the valley. Rosa and her husband, Rafael, soon suffered a series of misfortunes. Rafael injured his hand, which became infected and prevented him from working. The infection did not heal despite the use of many salves and prayers to God and the saints. Rosa began having frequent headaches. A large hole was burned in the family sofa by a lighted cigarette that had been left there. Next, three of Rosa's chickens died. Rosa says that Angela had enough money to help the family out of their financial difficulties but she refused to do so. She even refused to pay for her room and board. One evening, Rosa loudly condemned her daughter-in-law for her selfishness and implied she was an evil woman who slept with many men. Angela flew into a rage and slapped her mother-in-law. Before Rafael could rush to the aid of his wife, she grabbed a kitchen knife and stabbed Angela in the thigh. The girl fell screaming to the floor and blood flowed "as from a fountain." Rosa and Rafael bound the wound and tried to put the girl to bed but she packed her things and left threatening to go to the police. Apparently, she did not carry out her threat for the couple heard no more about the incident.

The day after Angela left, her in-laws realized that she had been a witch. Rafael's hand began to heal that very day and good things entered their lives again. Another son arrived home from a crop-picking trip and his accumulated wages rescued them from financial despair. "At once, I began to feel joy," Rosa said, "and my headaches disappeared. As soon as her blood began to flow I knew things would be better. When I saw how dark the blood was I knew this was no good woman my dead son had married. The blood was not red but dark and greasy. Had I known sooner, I would have cut her and saved us much grief. No doubt, she killed my son with her evil. If only we had known sooner"!

Identification of Witches

Such positive identification of a witch is rare. When a charge of witchcraft is made, it is usually done after the accused individual has left town or died, although rumors may circulate about someone who is generally disliked in the neighborhood. Open accusations of witchcraft are sometimes made against strangers whose peculiar behavior arouses suspicion. A Latin woman, a teacher, visiting in the valley during the course of sociological research was twice identified as a witch. As this teacher was getting off of a bus one day, a Mexican-American woman approached her saying she needed the services of a witch and had heard there was one in the neighborhood. She explained that an enemy had damaged her reputation by malicious gossip and she wanted to have the gossiper hexed as a form of self defense. Would the lady consent to send the hex for a reasonable fee? The teacher politely informed the local woman that she was not a witch and departed. On another occasion, this same teacher dropped a sack of orange peelings into a garbage can along the road in front of a house she was passing. A woman rushed out of the house screaming, "Witch! Witch! What do you have against us? Go back where you came from." She physically attacked the teacher, striking her about the face. The teacher tried in vain to reason with her but soon gave up and fled. Her attacker's brother apologized for the hostile behavior of his sister. The whole family had been embarrassed by her action, he told the teacher. "I do not believe in such superstitions," he said, "but my sister does so you must excuse her. I am a free-thinker, but you see, she is a Catholic as are our parents. You really must excuse her!"

The most powerful witches are said to live across the border in Mexico. The conservative Latins who believe that some hired witches live in Hidalgo County are either unable or unwilling to name them. Most witches are said to be women. One Mexican-American asserted:

> Only witches know the other witches. They hide their identity from the Christians and the police. And well they should. If we could name them, we would round them up and destroy them. They are Satan's children and our enemies. They worship Satan in groups and perform terrible rites. Some say they are Protestants but I think this is too broad a statement. I am sure that some Protestants are witches but the rest are not. They are merely misled.

Another Latin said:

> You should never ask where to find a witch. People will then know that you want to hire him to do someone harm. If you really want a witch you don't have to look for one. They sense the evil in your heart and they come to you. Many people hire witches to do harm to others. Some reason that this is alright for it is not they themselves who do the harm. But this is silly. One who hires a witch goes to hell as surely as the witch. One cannot blame the knife with which a man is killed. And killing with a knife is not as evil as witchcraft. A stabbing is clean. Witchcraft is evil and dirty and offends the soul as well as the body.

Motives

Despite general condemnation of the practice of witchcraft, conservative Latins of the lower classes maintain a nearly universal belief in the prevalence of witchcraft. Most cases of bewitchment are said to stem from a neighbor or acquaintance who wants to repay a personal offense. He supposedly seeks out a witch and pays him to do the harm.

It is said that a good person has nothing to fear from witches for they can harm only those who have done wrong. The respected elders of a folk community are believed to be relatively safe from witchcraft because they carefully observe the rules of good behavior and social distance designed to avoid giving offense. An old Latin farmer put it this way, "Witches cannot harm the good. A pure person who has followed God's way is safe from them. A witch cannot affect flesh that is pure. But each sin puts a bit of evil in a man. It is through this evil that the witches work. If you have no sin in you, then you are safe." "But," he added sadly, "where can you find a member of *La Raza* who has not at some time sinned? It is our fate."

The motives for witchcraft reflect the main areas of social friction in Mexican-American life. Envy is said to be the most common motive for witchcraft. Any display of material success followed by illness or tragedy may be thought to have aroused the envy of a friend or neighbor who arranged for the bewitchment. Fear of bewitchment motivated by envy is most pronounced among members of the lower-middle class who have accepted the Anglo goal of economic advancement.

Pedro, the owner of a small farm, celebrated his purchase of a pick-up truck by taking his friends to a bar. With the lubricating effect of the beer, he began to brag about how much more money he would make with the truck. A few days later, he became very ill and had to stay in bed for a month. In retrospect, he thought that he had behaved improperly in the bar. The *curandero* who came to the house to treat him was sure that he had been bewitched by an envious friend. A dead toad found in Pedro's doorway provided the *curandero* with absolute proof that his diagnosis was correct.

Sexual jealousy is also cited as a common motive for witchcraft. A woman may want to hex another female merely because she is more beautiful. Usually, the charge of witchcraft comes from an individual involved in an amatory triangle. The wife who thinks she is losing her husband to another woman may blame her for causing the trouble through witchcraft.

Vengeance for a real or felt offense is a third reason given for witchcraft. A proper man does not stoop to such base means of obtaining revenge. However, the man who thinks he has been bewitched may be so angry that he sees a suspect as being anything but proper and finds him guilty of hiring a witch to achieve revenge.

The actual mechanics of performing a hex are rarely clear because there are no witnesses except witches. Image magic is thought to be the most common technique. Illness is said to be caused by sticking pins in a doll resembling the victim or burying a photograph of the victim while reciting evil incantations. A witch can also produce sickness by sending worms into the body of the victim. Between jobs, the witch keeps his "Satanic worms" in a bottle of milk, according to one story. Some Mexican-Americans say that a witch can send a ghost or a demon to frighten the victim and make him fall ill with *espanto.* It is believed that a few witches can conjure up the victim's image in a glass of water and "freeze" his soul there. One old lady said, "Witches don't have to do anything in order to harm a person. They merely think and wish evil against someone and misfortune befalls him."

Treatment of Bewitchment

Bewitchment is often difficult to diagnose because it comes in many forms and positive symptoms may not show up until the disease has reached an advanced stage. A diagnosis of witchcraft may be made only after other diagnoses have been abandoned because the disease failed to respond to treatment by relatives, doctors, and *curanderos.* Any chronic or unexplained illness or misfortune is apt to be attributed to witchcraft. Mental illnesses are almost always associated with bewitchment. Symptoms include aberrant and erractic behavior, delusions, hallucinations, constant fear, and a feeling of being hated. Extreme nervousness and insomnia may be symptoms of bewitchment or fright. A deformed infant is sometimes regarded as an indication that the mother was bewitched during pregnancy.

Bewitchment is best treated by identifying the witch and forcing him to remove the hex. Although the victim may think he knows who hexed him, he usually seeks the services of a specialist to divine the identity of the witch. Sometimes, the witch can be forced to lift his spell by magical means rather than by personal confrontation. Such countermagic against the witch is supposedly performed only by specialists. Some of the older Latins say that only another witch can cure bewitchment. Others say that this disease can be cured in Mexico by practitioners who combine the arts of curing and witchcraft. In recent decades, the Magic Valley has seen the rise of a flourishing business in the treatment of bewitchment by spiritist and spiritualist curers who have a large Latin clientele. These expensive curers are said to have many unholy powers enabling them to combat witches.

If the witch who caused an illness cannot be identified, the next best procedure is to locate and destroy the magical paraphernalia used for the hex. The bewitchment tool may be a dead toad or bat, an image full of pins, a handful of grave dirt, or an unholy inscription on a piece of paper. A Mexican-American said he recovered from a bewitchment when his brother destroyed a crucifix wrapped in snakeskin found in the back yard. Another victim blamed his illness on a piece of paper bearing his name in red ink above some strange, cabalistic designs. He found the paper under the front seat of his car.

Many of these concepts of magical techniques come from the flood of books on black magic imported from Mexico. To what extent these books have produced a do-it-yourself form of the evil art is unknown but many are sold and discussed among close friends in the Mexican-American community. Amulets and prayers are also sold to protect the individual from bewitchment or cure him of the disease. Those who think they are in danger of being bewitched often rely on such protective devices but rarely believe them effective in curing bewitchment.

Curers and Witches

When Anglos and anglicized Latins talk about witchcraft beliefs, they tend to lump curers and witches together in the same category. It is becoming increasingly common to hear middle- and upper-class Latins refer to *curanderos* as *brujos* or witches. The *curanderos* are horrified by this label and deny the implication that they practice witchcraft. Some of them even refuse to treat bewitchment cases lest they be suspected of possessing evil powers. Others attempt to cure bewitchment with cleansings but will not perform counter-magic against the witch.

Respected *curanderos* take great pains to avoid discussions and books concerning the evil art. Such avoidance was demonstrated in a bookburning incident involving a well-known *curandera* named Doña Carmelita. Although she could not read, the *curandera* treasured two old "holy books" she had received from her grandmother. The books contained stories of early Christian saints and martyrs as well as creeds and prayers used in Mexican curing. When she heard that her friend, Mrs. Lopez, was going to Mexico, the *curandera* asked her to purchase new copies of the two books because her old ones were frayed. The *curandera* wanted the books purchased at a particular church in Mexico City because she had heard the books there were printed on parchment of human skin. Mrs. Lopez did not find the books on sale at the church but bought cheap, modern editions at a book store. On her return to the valley, she presented both volumes to *Doña* Carmelita. The *curandera* examined the first book, kissed it, and made the sign of the cross over it. Then, she picked up the second book displaying a red drawing of Satan on the cover. She dropped the book to the floor as though it had burned her fingers and raised both hands toward heaven. "In the name of God and Holy Mary," she called out. She placed both hands over the fallen book with her thumbs crossed over the index fingers and cried, "Leave here Satan in the name of the Father, the Son, and the Holy Ghost."

Mrs. Lopez tried to convince *Doña* Carmelita that the cover picture was merely a modern addition that in no way affected the contents of the book. She even showed the *curandera* that the old and new editions were identical, passage by passage. The *curandera* remained unconvinced. She led her friend into the garden where she built a fire with paper and added some herbs. Returning to the house, she delicately picked up the offensive book between two fingers, carried it outdoors, and dropped it on the fire. As the book burned, the *curandera* recited a prayer of purification. When the book had turned to ashes, the two women went indoors where the *curandera* sprinkled herself and her friend with blessed water. Finally, the two women sat down for a cup of coffee.

Doña Carmelita said:

> You must realize that anything that has had contact with Satan is evil. His image can even soil a holy book. Satan sends all evil and witchcraft is his loathsome plaything. Even I who am blessed by God to cure, even I fear that Evil One. I will treat bewitchment cases but I dread them and always purify myself afterwards. I like to avoid any sight, contact, or thought of Satan for even these things can endanger me. I must protect my precious ability to cure, which rests on my purity. The gift I have received from God is holy. I must not endanger this gift by exposing it to filth and evil.[1]

[1] These are literal translations from the Spanish, which is characteristically flowery.

10

Curers and Physicians

Divine Election of *Curanderos*

THE AGED *curandero* endowed with a gift from God has great prestige in Latin folk society where he is addressed with the respect term Don or *Doña* preceding the first name. Some *curanderos* do not realize their divine power until late in life but others sense it at an early age. In rare instances, a child with unusual powers gains recognition, particularly among those who rely on spiritualist curing.

Such a child is twelve-year-old Juanita. She works with an older curer who performs the actual treatment. Juanita's main role lies in her power to communicate "the word of the Lord." Standing before the patient, Juanita stares into his eyes. Her own eyelids slowly close and she begins to speak in a strange voice. She announces the nature of the illness and the steps required for treatment. Juanita's case is exceptional for even when divine power is recognized early in life, professional status is rarely attained before middle age. Due to the value placed on age and experience, Latins generally prefer an older *curandero* to a gifted but inexperienced youngster.

Doña Felicia is a highly respected *curandera* who was blessed with her divine gift during childhood but did not become a professional curer until her late forties. She told the story of her power:

> When I was a small child of six or seven, I had a lovely dog and I was very fond of him. One day, he was struck by a car and lay dead on the street. I rushed weeping and hysterical to pick up my pet and sat on the curb with my tears falling on his little face. My mother tried to comfort me and lead me into the house but I shook off her hands and said, "Let me alone!" My dear mother replied, "You must accept this. It is God's way." I sobbed, "How can God be so cruel. You said he loves us and now he has taken my baby's life. If God is good, he will cure my dog." As my tears fell on the dog, I

suddenly felt a oneness with his little body. I felt I was in it and I saw his little soul was still there. I felt a wave of power and love go through me. I knew I could awaken his soul. I said, "All Powerful God, wake up the soul of my little friend. Let me live." As I said these words, the dog moved a little and then opened his eyes. I stroked the hurt from his body as I laughed through my tears. My beloved mother fell to her knees beside me and said in a strange and quivering voice, "It is a miracle! You have brought back the dead." Later she said, "How God must love you!"

All our neighbors came to see the dog during the next few days and marveled. A week later I was asked to cure a sick chicken that belonged to my aunt. I took the chicken and didn't know what to do. I felt nothing but I saw that it's bill was open and it was gasping. Then I felt a voice say, "Look in its throat." I saw a fish bone stuck in the chicken's throat with dirt and a piece of string stuck to the bone. I took some tweezers and removed the blockage and the chicken recovered. In the months that followed, people with headaches and pains came and asked me to pray for them and rub their foreheads with my little hands. I could remove their pain.

My mother took me to see the priest to ask him what best use could be made of my gifts. She was a faithful churchgoer and relied entirely on the priest's advice. She was told that what had happened reflected my love of God but could not really be called miraculous. The priest said that my own health would be endangered if I were allowed to cure. My mother refused to believe that I lacked the holy gift but did not want me to be endangered so I stopped curing on her orders.

When I married, I became friendly with my husband's aunt who knew how to cure. She knew of my experiences and told me I should begin curing again. She began to teach me the techniques that God had revealed to her. She said she could teach only those who were blessed by God's touch. I learned the right prayers, how to bless water, and the herbs which God blessed with curing power. I learned the illnesses and how they manifested themselves. I learned how to take *susto* out of a person's body and how to relieve other sufferings. As my skills grew, I felt my old powers returning. But I only cured members of my own family and my friends.

Then my husband went north to pick crops and did not return. Someone told me he was living with another woman but I prayed to learn the truth and found that he was dead. A voice that I felt but did not hear said, "I have done this to free you so you can use my gift. It is not a punishment and your husband is in peace. I have sent you no children because I want you to use this gift. You have not used it freely before because of other obligations. Now you are free to cure and remove evil from the world. Share your blessing with others. Through you, I will cure."

I mourned my husband for several months but told a few women friends of my message. They urged me to use my gift. I bought many holy images for my altar and studied holy books. I prayed many hours every day. And then the sick began to come to my door. I am happy that I have overcome much pain and suffering. But I am humble for I am only an instrument of our Lord.

The gift of curing may be revealed through a dream, a vision, a voice, or merely a deep understanding of the sick. The revelation is frequently associated with a grave illness suffered by the gifted individual or a member of his family. A male curer received his gift during a pilgrimage to a distant shrine where he gave thanks for his daughter's recovery from a critical illness. As he knelt before the altar, he felt pain and great weariness from the long trip. He looked up at the altar and said, "But, I would suffer anything to repay your blessedness in curing my daughter." At that moment, his pain and fatigue vanished. "My body was suddenly filled with strength and joy," the curer recalled. "I saw an added brightness around the altar and felt a cool, loving pressure on my head. And I heard a voice say, 'It is through you that I cured your daughter. You have my power within you. If you wish to truly repay me, use this gift to help the sick and suffering."

There can be little doubt about the sincerity of most *curanderos* in their belief that they are chosen by God to help the sick. Very few of them make any substantial profit from curing. The majority work at other tasks and cure only in their spare time. Most *curanderos* do not charge fees. The patient is expected to leave an offering of about fifty cents on the curandero's altar to pay for candles burned in honor of a saint throughout the course of treatment. It is also customary for the patient to bring the *curandero* small gifts, such as a chicken, a basket of vegetables, or the cash equivalent if he can afford it, but cash is not required for treatment. The total cost of treatment by the *curandero* is estimated to be about one dollar per visit, which is indeed reasonable compared to the physician's fee.

Most of the traditional curers feel that their divine gifts would be withdrawn if they were to demand payment for their services. One *curandero* said, "My reward is in being close to God. I cure for love and not to become rich. Do you think God would allow me to take money from the poor? Riches come to those who worship Satan. Salvation is the reward of those who adore the Lord."

Modernization of Curing

Such contempt for monetary rewards is notably lacking among the ever increasing numbers of spiritist and spiritualist healers. Some of them have studied spirit curing at temples in Mexico and received certificates, which hang on their walls. These certificates can also be obtained through correspondence courses administered by spiritist centers in Mexico City. The students are trained to summon up spirits of the dead who diagnose illness and prescribe treatment. On the completion of their formal training, these curers treat illness only for fixed fees payable in advance. Their fees are frequently higher than those charged by physicians.

Although the traditional *curanderos* scorn the fee system, they have adopted other practices from modern medicine. It is becoming quite common for *curanderos* to give their patients written prescriptions for herb medicines. These prescriptions are usually filled at drug stores across the border where the medicine is put in bottles or boxes with typed labels. A few *curanderos* give injections of vitamins or penicillin. Antibiotics can be purchased without prescription at drug stores in Mexico where druggists instruct the curer in the technique of giving hypodermic injections and tell him the standard dosages. Mexican-Americans have a high regard for injections because of their rapid results. Patients often pride themselves on utilizing *curanderos* "who know modern medicine" as well as folk medicine. "Why should I pay a big fee to an Anglo physician merely to get the same prescription and some worthless advice?" one Mexican-American asked.

Several *curanderos* maintain consulting rooms equipped with medical instruments and bottles of drug store medicines arranged on a table near the altar. One of these curers uses a stethoscope to listen to the patient's heartbeat.

The growing number of innovations in curing has made the conservative Mexican-Americans suspicious that a new or unknown curer may be a quack *(carancho)* who is out to make money by duping the public. Any curer who charges a fixed fee is suspect. The spiritualist curers are particularly suspect because of their high fees, but they have established a reputation for being able to cure bewitchment. It is considered unwise to consult an unknown curer unless he has been recommended by close friends or respected acquaintances. Even then, the prospective patient may first test the curer by asking him indirect questions in order to gain some insight into his qualifications and knowledge. A healer who fails to perform successful cures is soon labeled as a quack in the Mexican-American community. He loses his clientele and may be run out of town. Patients who think they have been cheated by a "fake *curandero*" sometimes complain to the police. The complaint is usually made on the grounds that the impostor is a crook who has no divine power. Police investigation may result in a charge of fraud or practicing medicine without a license.

The reputation of a *curandero* can also be ruined by the death of a patient during the course of treatment. Moreover, such a disaster is likely to lead to a legal investigation and criminal charges. For these reasons, most *curanderos* refuse to accept cases that they regard as terminal. They advise the patient of their inability to treat his illness and often refer him to a doctor. One female curer takes the patient by taxi to a hospital. Thus, the *curandera* is relieved of possible moral and legal responsibility for a death. This policy also reinforces the folk belief that the hospital is "a place where people die."

Traditional curers may be either general practitioners or specialists. A number of female curers are licensed midwives. Others specialize in the treatment of fright sickness. The *hueseros* (bone healers) used to set broken limbs but today fractures are treated by physicians. The remaining bone healers now treat sprains, aches, and muscular weakness by massage and realignment of muscles or tendons that have "gotten out of place." A skilled *huesero* is regarded as capable even if he has not received a divine gift for curing. Some *curanderos* specialize in certain techniques such as curing with blessed water. Specialists in divination are consulted in cases where the patient has not responded to treatment by *curanderos* or physicians.

The technique of curing are learned in different ways. Many of the older *curanderos* say they were instructed through divine revelation. Some have served an apprenticeship under an established practitioner in Texas or Mexico. The spiritualists and spiritists learn their curing methods from books, lectures, demonstrations, and mediumistic contacts.

Relationships with Curers and Doctors

The relationship between the respected *curandero* and his patient is warm and intimate. The patient is not treated merely as an individual but as a member of a family unit. To the Latin, illness is always a matter of family concern. The *curandero* shares his diagnosis with the family and carefully explains each step of the treatment. It is customary for at least one member of the family to accompany the patient to the curer's home, and family members are often asked to aid the curer in administering the treatment. Throughout the period of treatment, a very close and affective relationship is maintained between the curer, the patient, and the patient's family. Never does the curer say he is too busy to sit down and discuss the ailment with the patient and his family. The *curandero* openly suffers with the patient when he experiences pain and rejoices with him when the signs of recovery appear.

José compared the relationship shared with a *curandero* and physician:

> Both curer and doctor are specialists in curing illness. The curer can treat some diseases and the doctor knows how to treat other afflictions. But the way they feel is always different. A curer cares about the patient and not about the fee. A doctor explains nothing and struts about as though he were a great man and you were only a fool. If you pay a doctor, he doesn't care whether you live or die. The curer cares. Have you ever seen a doctor grieve because of pain you suffer? Have you ever had one comfort you? Or respect you? A curer cures because he cares. The doctor cures because he likes money and power.
>
> The curer respects everyone but the doctor respects only himself. The curer will send you to a doctor when you have a sickness he can cure. Once when I thought I had *empacho,* I went to a curer. He felt my belly and said it was not *empacho* but something bad in there that must come out. He sent me to a doctor and I went to a hospital and my appendix was cut out. A curer admits there are things he cannot cure and helps you find someone to treat it. Have you ever had a doctor send you to a curer because your sickness was *susto?* Doctors know they can't treat *susto.* But they say it is some other disease and give you worthless medicine until you die. And you pay right to the end. Then they sign a certificate saying some disease killed you and they think they are free of blame.

The Mexican-Americans are highly sensitive to behavior of the physician, which seems to reflect a feeling of unwarranted superiority over other men. A physician may receive some respect for his formal training but the Mexican-American often feels that the doctor has not learned enough. This opinion is reinforced when there is any delay or indecision in the diagnosis. Ignacio contrasted the diagnostic procedures of the physician and the *curandero:*

> When I see a curer, I tell him what probably caused my illness and list my symptoms. He talks with me about my suffering and looks into my eyes. He may clean me with an egg to see whether it pulls anything out of my body. But very quickly he knows what is wrong with me. The doctors know less. I went to a doctor with great pain in my stomach especially when I was hungry. He made me drink an awful white drink and then took x-rays of my stomach. Imagine having to take pictures to see what is inside a person? A curer knows that without having to look inside you with machines or running to look in a book. Many doctors act as though they know everything but I can tell you that very few are qualified. The curers know more.

The Mexican-American is insulted when his self-diagnosis is dismissed by the physician or denounced as superstition. Mr. Montoya took his wife to a physician after she had failed to respond to treatment by a *curandero.* He had been talked into this visit by his older brother who had been successfully treated by the doctor. Mr. Montoya was enraged by the experience:

> We saw the doctor in his office after a long wait while many Anglos went in first. The doctor asked my wife, "What is wrong"? I told him. I said my wife had no energy and often had no appetite. I told him how she had bad dreams and cried in her sleep. I explained that she must have *susto* but had not responded to the treatment of a *curandero.* Therefore, she must have *susto pasado.* I said I had come to him because my brother thought he could probably cure this disease. The doctor sat there smiling as I talked. When I finished, he laughed at me. Then he sat up straight and said sternly, "Forget all that nonsense. You have come to me and I will treat your wife. It is my job to decide what is wrong with her. And forget about those stupid superstitions. I don't know how a grown man like you can believe such nonsense!" He treated me like a fool. And then he really insulted me. He said, "Mr. Montoya, if you will please step into the waiting room, I will examine your wife." As I rose, he said to Carmelita, "Step over there and take off your clothes." This I would not stand, that my wife should be naked with this man. And he said this in front of me. I controlled myself and only said, "Come, Carmelita, we have no time now." The doctor said, "Okay, but make an appointment with the nurse for her to come in for an examination." And the lecherous goat added, "Mr. Montoya, you do not have to come with her every time." We never returned, of course, and my wife was treated by a curer. Maybe Anglos let doctors stare at their wives' bodies and fool with them but not me. And the fool did not even know about *susto.* He is lucky I did not reduce his arrogance right there.

The "immodesty" of the physical examination alienates many Latins. A curer would never think of asking a member of the opposite sex to disrobe. The physical contact between curer and patient is kept at a minimum and is always carried out with care to protect the patient's feelings and modesty.

Objections to Modern Medicine

The physician's diagnosis is phrased in scientific terms that the lower-class Latin does not understand or even attempt to understand. Unless the response to treatment is rapid, the Latin patient will terminate his relationship with the physician and try another doctor, *curandero,* or home remedy. Julio is a case in point:

> I went to this doctor because of pains in my chest when I breathed. He took pictures and blood from me and said it was not too serious. He said he could cure me. He gave me the long name of some disease. I did everything he told me to do except quit smoking. But four days later, I was no better. It is obvious that the doctor didn't know what he was doing. I said to my wife that I would stop seeing him and would not renew the prescription for the medicine. Her aunt rubbed my chest with herbs and lard and the next day I was better.

Credit for a cure produced by modern medicine is frequently attributed to folk treatments that preceded, accompanied, or followed scientific treatment. Magdalena, the daughter of a lower-class family, had been complaining of exhaustion, aches, and fear. When she started running a high fever accompanied by frequent chills, her mother took her to a *curandera.* The curer began the treatment for *espanto* as Magdalena said she had seen the ghost of her dead uncle. Meanwhile, her father had consulted his compadre about the matter and reluctantly followed his advice to take the girl to a hospital. During the five days that Magdalena was treated for a virus disease in the hospital, her mother and the curer prayed for her recovery. They found a photograph of the dead uncle and sprinkled it with wet herbs that had been dipped in blessed water. Together, they begged the ghost to go away and stop frightening Magdalena. When the girl returned from the hospital, the explanations of her recovery varied. The compadre cited her cure as absolute proof of the soundness of modern medicine. Her mother said the hospitalization was unnecessary since the cure was due to the pacification of the ghost. Her father wavered between these two explanations. A month later he said:

> Both treatments contributed to my daughter's recovery. There can be no doubt that her body was ill and the doctors made her more comfortable by killing the *animalitos.* But the doctors treat the body as though it were a machine. They forget about the soul. It was the ghost of my wife's brother that frightened her and weakened her so the bugs could make her sick. If the curer had not laid my brother's soul to rest, the same thing would have happened again.

Except in a crisis, hospitalization is avoided like a plague. To be separated from the family and isolated in an Anglo world is well-nigh intolerable for the conservative Mexican-American. Next to prison, the hospital is most dreaded as a place of isolation in an impersonal and enigmatic world. The Mexican-American patient often has no one to talk to in hospitals, which enforce strict rules prohibiting Latin nurses from speaking Spanish on the premises. Hospitalization can become a nightmarish experience when surgery is involved for the Mexican-American thinks there is something ungodly about cutting out parts of a living body.

Timo recalled with horror his successful operation in a modern hospital:

> I was alone in a room with many other patients who did not know me or care about me. Except for one, the nurses pretended not to know Spanish. That one nurse was kind and if it had not been for her I would have gone mad. She explained what would happen and soothed my fears. She also explained why my family could not stay with me but only visit me briefly. She told me not to be afraid because God was everywhere even if no one in the hospital loved Him enough to put up a picture of His Son. She told me that no one died from my type of operation and she knew many of *La Raza* who had been cured by being cut. She sensed my fear of not being whole after this thing was cut from me. So she explained that the thing to be removed was evil and not a part of a whole and healthy body. Then I felt better. She was good, that nurse. But even she could not explain the scandal of the food we had to eat. Twice she looked away when my wife smuggled me some tortillas and other food that God intended for man.

An understanding Anglo nurse made this comment on the hospital situation, "It's a shame that the dogma and ritual of modern medicine won't allow us to make a comfortable environment for the Latin patient. It would be so easy but so heretical."

Latin objections to hospitalization also apply to isolation in T.B. sanatoriums. Some tubercular patients say they would rather die at home than live away from their families in a sanatorium. Resistance to modern medical treatment for tuberculosis is further increased by the belief that this disease is an advanced stage of *susto,* which is best treated by a *curandero.* Lower-class Latins seldom have faith in the scientific treatment for T.B. because it is so slow in effecting recovery.

Another barrier to Latin acceptance of modern medicine lies in the folk belief that illness sent by the will of God cannot be prevented by scientific techniques. Latin resistance to immunization programs constitutes a major problem for public-health workers in south Texas. Theories of preventative medicine presented in classes on prenatal care have not made much of an impression on the women of Latin folk society. Few of them see the connection between the birth of a healthy baby and prenatal care by a physician. Nor do they see the lack of prenatal care as a cause of infant mortality. When an infant dies at birth, the tragedy is accepted as the will of God.

Increasing Reliance on Physicians

In spite of their objections to modern medicine, Mexican-Americans are going to physicians for treatment of an increasing number of ailments.

Latin parents are particularly conscientious about taking sick children to the doctor when there is the slightest cause for alarm even though the cost of medical treatment may impose a severe financial strain on the family. Ailments that used to be diagnosed as evil eye or fright are now suspected of being influenza or colic. In doubtful cases, the family takes the sick member to both a physician and a curer. Generally, neither practitioner is aware that the other is also treating the patient.

Latin acceptance of modern medicine is based primarily on the empirical evidence of its efficacy provided by the miracle drugs. Education has produced some change in Latin medical beliefs but the modern ideas taught in elementary school rarely outweigh contrary parental teaching. Students who go on to junior and senior high school are more likely to reject the old-fashioned ideas of their parents and accept modern medicine. Veterans of the armed forces returned to civilian life convinced of the value of scientific medicine.

The social barrier between the Latin patient and the physician is being eased by a few understanding doctors and nurses. One physician never contradicts the self-diagnosis of his patients. Instead he says, "Perhaps, you are right so go ahead with the treatment for that disease. But just in case something else is involved, let us also use this treatment along with the other." When the patient recovers, he may ask the physician about the nature of the ailment and the cure. The doctor carefully explains in simple terms that the patient can understand and repeat to his family. The satisfied patients of this doctor become living advertisements for modern medicine.

Too often, however, Latin doctors are *inglesados* who look back on their own folk origins with contempt that is reflected in their relations with patients who cling to folk beliefs. These doctors are often more intolerant of unscientific thinking than Anglo doctors. The anglicized Latin doctor feels the patient's hostility and commonly answers it with satire. This response increases the communication barrier between patient and physician and heightens Latin resentment against a hostile and dominant Anglo society.

Today, the degree of reliance on modern medicine is correlated with class and education. The lower class depends on *curanderos* more than any other segment of society but uses modern medicine in addition to folk medicine. The lower-middle class manifests more skepticism about the techniques of folk curing but uses folk medicine in addition to modern medicine. The upper-middle class regards going to a physician as a matter of prestige but appeals to God are deemed essential for a cure. The members of this class are more apt to consider medical explanations of illness first and resort to folk explanations only when modern medical treatment has failed. The elite rely almost entirely on physicians and prayer. Only in the terminal stages of a fatal disease or in cases of inexplicable, chronic illness do they turn to a curer. Both middle and upper-class *inglesados* ridicule folk medicine and may even deny that any Mexican-Americans believe in *curanderismo.*

Belief in folk diseases probably will continue for many years in the Magic Valley. The reasons are several. Any conservative Latin can cite numerous cases of cures achieved by folk medicine. Many of these cases would have ended in recovery whether treated by modern medicine, *curanderismo,* or left untreated. However, the curer's knowledge of the sociocultural stresses underlying Latin ailments sometimes enables him to produce dramatic and real relief from psychosomatic illness. *Curanderos* have effected true recovery in several cases of mental illness that failed to respond to psychiatric treatment due to the psychiatrist's ignorance of the value conflicts and social stresses involved in Mexican-American ailments. In a real sense, *curanderismo* frequently cures.

11

Folk Psychotherapy

Resolution of Interpersonal Conflicts

THE FOLK DISEASES of *La Raza* are not listed in medical textbooks but they are real in the world of the conservative Mexican-American. When a Latin says he is sick with fright, he is really sick. Because the symptoms of each folk disease are so vague and diverse, it is impossible to categorically equate folk ailments with medically recognized diseases. A partial list of the symptoms of fright sickness would include: nervousness, insomnia, frightening dreams, uncontrolled weeping, burning eyes, muscular aches, and general malaise.

A folk disease is not always distinguished solely on the basis of symptoms. The diagnosis also rests on the nature of interpersonal conflicts recently experienced by the patient. Any ailment that follows a crisis in interpersonal relations is likely to be diagnosed as one of the folk diseases. The diagnosis and treatment fulfills valid functions in easing the sociocultural stresses involved in illness.

Sometimes a threatened crisis is avoided by a diagnosis of illness. Such was the case with Miguel, a Latin teen-ager. He had boasted to his age mates that he would "conquer" Margarita at a forthcoming dance. It was important for him to carry out this plan to prove his *machismo*. Retreat from his open declaration of intent would have "reduced" Miguel in the eyes of his friends. A few days later, he was stunned to discover that his elder brother had become interested in the same girl. For Miguel to proceed with his plan of seduction would be a serious affront to his brother. Caught in this dilemma, Miguel brooded. He could see no out from the hopeless situation. When illness struck him, it seemed like a blessing rather than a misfortune. The day before the dance, Miguel noticed stiffness and pain in his left leg. As the pain increased, he mentioned it to his parents. His mother examined Miguel and announced that he had *aire*. He was ordered to bed for twenty-four hours with a poultice of ground tomatoes and herbs over the stiff leg. Before the dance, his elder brother came to Miguel's bedside to wish him a rapid recovery.

A crisis involving similar conflict of Mexican values was averted when Memo developed a case of fright sickness. He had been fired by his Latin employer for repeated failure to show up for work. Memo was angry at the time, although much later he admitted to a friend that his employer's complaint was valid. After the firing, he went to a bar in search of consolation from friends and alcohol. The story he told his friends depicted Memo as a victim of great injustice. His drinking companions expressed approval of his plan to go back and have a showdown with his employer. The more Memo drank, the more he felt that he had been wronged. Then he announced that the very next day he would go to his ex-boss and demand reinstatement in his job. Alejandro, a fellow worker at the cannery plant that had employed Memo, said he would watch the showdown with pride in having such a friend. In the early hours of the morning, Memo started home happy in his resolve to "hold his own" against his "unfair" boss. En route, he tripped on a curbing and fell into the street where he narrowly missed being run over by a truck. When Memo awoke the next morning his body was filled with pain that reached a climax of agony in his head. His hands were shaky, his stomach unsettled, and an undefined anxiety haunted him. A neighbor known for her curing ability was called in to examine the patient. The ailment was defined as fright caused by the narrow escape from being killed by the truck. Memo was treated and ordered to remain in bed for several days. He postponed the showdown with his former boss and finally forgot about it. Thus, he was spared the necessity of showing disrespect to an elder who was a socially-respected employer. Such action would have met with disapproval from most of the community.

Social disapproval of an individual who has violated expected role behavior may subside if he is shown to be suffering from a folk disease. Bewitchment is held to be responsible for aberrant behavior, which would be severly condemned if it were performed willingly. Enrique violated the rules of proper behavior for a dutiful son but escaped the full consequences of his action by discovering that he had been bewitched.

To help his father move some furniture from an uncle's house, Enrique borrowed a truck from his cousin. On the way home with his load, he stopped to chat with Berta, an attractive girl known for her loose morals. At her suggestion, they drove to a restaurant for some beer and conversation. Enrique drank more than he intended and suddenly realized that he would be far overdue in delivering the furniture and returning the truck. He left Berta and sped homeward. His reckless driving caused the truck to skid off a curve and turn over on its side. Enrique was badly cut and much of the furniture was smashed. The police took the bleeding Latin to a hospital emergency ward where his wounds were treated. He was then returned home to face his father's wrath. After his father gave him a tongue lashing for his "stupid and irresponsible behavior," Enrique went to bed on his mother's orders. While his mother was washing his bloodstained clothes, she found a small ball of cloth pinned to his shirt. Inside the ball was a little chunk of clay with hair and knotted strings imbedded in it. This discovery provided evidence that Enrique had been bewitched by the evil Berta. The magical paraphernalia was sprinkled with lime and burned in a can by Enrique's father. His mother cleaned him by sprinkling his body with blessed water containing pieces of holy palm leaf. The transfer of responsibility from the son to a witch helped assuage the father's anger. Enrique's repentance for associating with a loose woman when he should have been working further pacified his father. Enrique promised that he would avoid Berta in the future. The next day he helped his father and cousin repair the truck and salvage the furniture that could be repaired. The charge of witchcraft had freed Enrique from much of the guilt for his rash behavior. Through family cooperation in removing the hex, he was reinstated as a loyal son.

Value Conflicts of Acculturated Patients

The cases just cited show how folk medicine eases social situations involving a conflict of values within Mexican-American folk culture. The value conflicts of the Mexican-American are multiplied with the acceleration of acculturation. Many individuals are caught in a dilemma involving the internalization of conflicting Anglo and Latin values. When this uncomfortable situation prevents the individual from achieving a sense of identity and community, he may attribute his anxieties and failures to witchcraft. Such was the case with Roberto who now uses this Spanish form of his name instead of Robert, as his parents call him.

He is the son of anglicized parents who fought their way up the economic ladder and completely identified with the Anglo world. They looked back with contempt at the conservative Latin world they had left behind. Their son was urged to earn high grades in school and eventually qualify for a profession.

Roberto attended schools where the majority of Latin students came from conservative, lower-class families. In these families, parents see little value in the academic success of their children. The lack of good job opportunities for Latins in Texas prevents them from viewing education as a means of occupational advancement. Parental indifference toward formal education is often reflected in the academic performance of Mexican-American pupils. Moreover, these students scorn competitive scholastic endeavor as an attempt to outdo and demean other students.

The student who enters this kind of school environment from an *inglesado* home faces a difficult task of adjustment. His family demands high grades and a future orientation. By trying to please his parents, he may alienate his Latin school mates and fail to gain acceptance among the Anglo students. If he conforms to the values of the lower-class, Mexican-American students, he meets parental outrage. Sometimes, the Latin student in this situation switches periodically from one alternative to the other as Roberto did.

For a long time, Roberto had done exceedingly well in high school. As a result, he had been without close friends. Then one semester, he flunked several courses. He did not know why he had done so badly but afterwards he was accepted by the Mexican-American students. His parents used both persuasion and coercion in their attempts to force Roberto to compete for high grades. Instead, he fell in love. He and his sweetheart approached their parents for permission to be married. Both families forbad the wedding. The obedient daughter refused to see Roberto again and his Latin friends scoffed him. A few days later, his face broke out with acne, which made him feel conspicuous and humiliated before the world. He sought help.

According to Roberto's story, he consulted a physician, a priest, and a psychiatrist. He said the physician could not help him and the priest only admonished him to have faith in God. The psychiatrist, according to Roberto, told him the only treatment he needed was to lose his virginity. Roberto himself came to the conclusion that he had been bewitched. Although he may have invented the story of the psychiatrist, Roberto was convinced that he had been hexed.

He made a 200-mile trip to Austin to see me because he had heard a TV program on which I discussed Renaissance Satanic witchcraft, and he thought I could help him. We talked for several hours but I had precious little advice to offer him. Later, I met a friend of his who told me that Roberto was being treated for bewitchment by a spiritualist curer. I know nothing about the treatment or its outcome but I doubt whether it was successful. He was caught in the no man's land between two cultures and felt that he did not belong in either the Anglo or the Latin community. Today, cases like Roberto's are becoming rare because there are enough *inglesado* students in most schools to form a subgroup of their own.

The adult who attempts cultural transfer from conservative Latin to Anglo society meets the same kind of problems that confronted Roberto. Acceptance in either society may be difficult or impossible to obtain. The *inglesado* is outcast by conservative Latin society and frequently refused acceptance by Anglo society. Some *inglesados* in this position redouble their efforts to achieve Anglo goals and Anglo acceptance. Others find the situation intolerable and seek retreat back into Mexican-American folk society. These individuals often experience repeated attacks of folk diseases, which constitute overt proof that at heart they are still members of *La Raza* because Anglos and *inglesados* are held to be immune from the folk diseases.

Social Outcasting and Reacceptance

The case of José illustrates the processes of outcasting and reacceptance by Mexican-American folk society. In his mid-twenties, José lived with his poor but respected parents. Two years of high school and a term in the army inspired him to try for economic advancement. Electrical training in the army and an apprenticeship in a radio-TV shop qualified him as a repairman. He was soon making good money. Following Latin tradition, he turned most of his income over to his father for rent, food, and the debt he owed him for his upbringing.

The trouble began when José aspired to be an automobile owner. His income could accommodate the time payments only if he ceased turning money over to his father. As his parents were nursing a sick daughter, they refused his request to use the funds for the purchase of a car. Unfortunately, José had announced to his friends that he would soon be the owner of an automobile. Failure to procure the vehicle would, he felt, lower his worth and dignity in the eyes of his friends. After an argument with his parents, he left home and was soon driving a second-hand Ford.

Only two members of José's *palomilla* owned cars and his was the finest by far. His newly-acquired automobile and extra spending money made him more attractive to girls, although most conservative parents refused to let their daughters go out with him because he had deserted his family. Soon José's friends began to resent his display of opulence, and he began to suspect that people were gossiping about his violation of filial obligations.

In an attempt to maintain his self-image as a successful man, José began to cultivate Anglo mannerisms in both Anglo and Latin social environments. He also became lax in the observation of Mexican-American etiquette. One day he went too far. When he arrived at the Arriega house to pick up a radio for repairs, he found no one at home but the teen-age daughter. He dallied to chat with her in violation of the custom that no proper girl should be left unchaperoned with a man. Mrs. Arriega walked in and thought she heard José making an improper proposition to her daughter. The mother screamed accusations that drove José from the house without the radio. The story of the incident spread rapidly. Together with his desertion of his parents, this scandal ruined José's reputation. He was labeled as an *inglesado* and a beast.

José's services as a repairman were requested less and less. His income fell. After he missed several payments on his car, it was repossessed. His social relations were limited by now to a few drinking companions. Wherever he went, he began to feel the presence of an evil force that was taking over control of his behavior. Twice he suffered periods of memory loss after leaving a bar. José decided that he was ill and consulted a *curandero*. After a prolonged consultation, the *curandero* informed José that he had been bewitched. He said that if José had not violated his sacred trust to his parents, his spirit would have been strong enough to resist the evil sent upon him. The curse could not be lifted until this breech of familial relations had been repaired, the *curandero* added.

José approached his parents with apologies and requested permission to return home. His father refused and ordered him to leave the house. Later, his mother accompanied José to see the *curandero*. She found out that the curer had learned the name of the person responsible for the hex. The guilty one was the Arriega girl who had long desired José's affections and felt offended by his failure to reciprocate. Somewhere, the curer said, there was a doll made of José's image and wrapped in the girl's undergarments. When the doll was destroyed, José would be free of the evil. José's mother told her husband about the diagnosis and repeated the story to her closest female friends. The father remained displeased but allowed José to return home.

Two days later, the curer announced that he had discovered the hex image and burned it. José underwent several purification rites and his relations with his father improved. His old *palomilla,* panting with curiosity for details, picked José up one evening for a session of beer drinking. The evil force controlling him was now laid completely to rest. He accompanied his family on a crop-picking journey and returned home a loyal member of *La Raza.*

Mariá also was outcast and later reaccepted by the folk community. She had been happily married to Fernando for five years before her troubles began. María had given birth to a healthy baby and was pleased that her friend Emilia agreed to become the child's godmother. The relationship between the two friends was close before María began to feel envy of her *comadre* whose husband obtained a promotion to the position of foreman at a considerable increase in salary. His monetary gain was reflected in Emilia's new wardrobe and the new automobile they acquired. María regarded such a conspicuous display of wealth as improper but could not help envying her friend. At the same time, María's financial resources dwindled because her husband had begun an extramarital affair and showered his mistress with gifts. María wanted to take a job to augment their income but her husband refused to give her permission. He announced with dignity that he was capable of providing for his family. The relationship between husband and wife deteriorated until they voiced open expressions of anger in the home. When Fernando went north to pick crops, María refused to accompany him on the grounds that their child was too sick to travel. Fernando's eldest sister moved in with María after her husband left.

After Fernando's departure, María got a job as a store clerk in a nearby town. During her working hours, Fernando's sister took care of María's child. Both the sister and Emilia urged María to quit her job and cease disobeying her husband. María ignored their advice and worked harder to make more money. She began to attend evening classes at a secretarial school. Once she told her *comadre* that she would desert Fernando if he remained obstinate on his return. She assured Emilia that she could make more money as a secretary than her uneducated husband could possibly earn. As María sensed the hostility of her conservative friends, she began to flaunt them by displaying anglicized mannerisms. Resentment of her behavior grew and her own parents began to withhold their usual expressions of love when she visited them. Her mother wept for her and gossip spread about her openly-declared decision to be a "free woman."

One day María was alarmed to hear that her husband had learned about her behavior and was on his way home. The same evening she went to a mixed party at the home of an anglicized girl she had met at the secretarial school. Word spread that María drank too much at the party and behaved in "outrageous" ways. The next morning she began menstruating and noted an abnormally heavy flow of blood. She experienced nausea, unsteadiness, and a feeling that her bones were pliable. Her body seemed to be "on fire" and she perspired freely. Then she began to weep and became almost hysterical. Her sister-in-law tried to relieve her with teas, aspirin, and an oil massage but María's condition became worse. She moaned that she was bewitched and was going to die.

Her mother and mother-in-law came to María soon after they were called. They listened to her self-diagnosis and observed that her symptoms were serious. Both mothers rushed off to see their husbands and obtained permission to take María to a curer. Through her suffering, María had been returned to her family. It would be the curer's job to restore her to health. The treatment would also return her to folk society.

The two older women took María by taxi to the home of *Doña* Iñes, a famous and respected *curandera. Doña* Iñes listened to the girl's complaints and her self-diagnosis of bewitchment. The details about María's private life that emerged during the conversation reenforced the curandera's knowledge of the case obtained through channels of female gossip. *Doña* Iñes filled a glass with blessed water and slowly passed it back and forth over María's head. The surface of the water formed ripples indicating that the liquid was "rejecting" María. The *curandera* left the women to be alone so she could commune with God. When she returned, her face registered grief at the diagnosis she was about to pronounce. It was *castigo de Dios* (a punishment from God) for María's violation of her obligation to her husband, her child, and her parents.

Due to the gravity of this affliction, *Doña* Iñes requested María to remain in her home for treatment. The patient's mother and sister-in-law agreed to take care of María's child for the duration of the illness. The *curandera* gave María herbal teas and massages but her main treatment consisted of prayer. For many hours a day, María knelt in prayer in front of the *curandera's* altar. *Doña* Iñes frequently talked with María about her illness and gently showed her the error of her ways. She made María realize that she must pay for her sins and repent before she could be cured. As the enormity of her sins became clear to her, María was filled with remorse. In her agony, she wept for hours. Food became distasteful and sleep fitful or full of nightmares.

María's fear knew no bounds when she heard that her husband had returned and conferred daily with the curer. The nature of the discussions between the curer and the husband were kept secret from the patient. *Doña* Iñes informed Fernando of his wife's sins but emphasized the fact that he was not free of guilt. She said that María might not have been led astray if her husband had given her more love and comfort. The *curandera* implied that Fernando had shown more interest in pleasure than duty. God had noticed his shortcomings, she added. *Doña* Iñes had arranged for Fernando's mother to be present at her daily session with him. His awareness that his own mother knew his shortcomings prevented Fernando from trying to throw all the blame on his wife.

At last, *Doña* Iñes felt that the time had come for María and her husband to face each other. She arranged the meeting before her altar but forbad the couple to speak until after they had knelt together in prayer. The *curandera* blessed them with water and prayed aloud for their return to a state of blessedness in the eyes of the Lord. With bowed head, she stated that God intended man to live with his wife. "A man is because of woman and a woman is because of her man," she concluded. *Doña* Iñes raised the couple to their feet and María humbly begged her husband's forgiveness. Fernando chose not to answer but allowed María to accompany him home. Slowly their relations became more friendly and together they made a pilgrimage to offer their thanks at a holy shrine. Today María is humble. Her mannerisms and dress are subdued. Fernando is still proving his *machismo* by pursuing other women but he shows tender affection for his wife and buys her gifts from time to time. Their current behavior conforms to the expectations of Mexican-American folk society.

Treatment of Mental Illness

Curanderos have cured several cases of mental illness that previously failed to respond to psychiatric treatment in modern hospitals. In these cases, the failure of modern medical science stemmed from the psychiatrist's ignorance of the world view and value system of the conservative Mexican-American. The case of Catalina illustrates the importance of such cultural factors in the rehabilitation of the Latin patient.

When she was twenty years old, Catalina had been committed to the state mental hospital as a paranoid patient. Her parents were reluctant to sign the commitment order because they feared Anglo institutions and disliked abandoning their responsibility to personally care for a sick member of the family. They later used every means at their disposal to obtain their daughter's release. No improvement was noted in Catalina's condition after two years of treatment and she was released in the custody of her parents. As soon as she returned home, her parents placed her under the care of a curer.

The treatment that Catalina received under the curer's care would be regarded as barbaric by most psychiatrists but it was successful. When she had won the confidence of her patient, the *curandera* learned that Catalina believed the world hated her because she had committed a sexual perversion with an Anglo during her teens. She was laden with guilt and self-recrimination. On hearing Catalina's confession, the *curandera* registered emotions of horror and disgust. "No wonder everybody hates you!" she exclaimed, "God hates you too." It was only natural, the *curandera* continued, for God to send hatred for such a sinner into the hearts of all. The *curandera* did not conceal her own contempt for Catalina but announced that she would help the girl because it was her duty to God who had given her the power to cure.

The treatment consisted of a painful program of penance and self-debasement accompanied by prayer. Catalina was allowed to wear only the dark color of mourning and she was required to spend hours on her knees praying for forgiveness. When the *curandera* discovered Catalina's fondness for the rabbits her father raised, the patient was ordered to cut open the head of a rabbit every morning and eat the raw brains from the skull. This act caused Catalina extreme anguish and considerable nausea. Aside from the rabbit brains, the patient was kept on a rigid and tasteless diet. She was denied permission to indulge in any frivolous or pleasurable activity. To complete her miserable existence, the patient was ordered to report for regular floggings at the home of the *curandera.*

The *curandera* never revealed the nature of Catalina's sin to anyone else for had it been known the girl would have been outcast forever from respectable society. Instead, the *curandera* leaked out the information that Catalina was being punished for failure to demonstrate the proper respect for her parents. As the story spread, many listeners felt that the penance imposed on Catalina was too severe. Women who knew her went out of their way to demonstrate their friendliness and respect to Catalina for the suffering she had endured to repair the injury to her parents. Catalina came to believe that she was no longer hated by everybody. The *curandera* became more and more affective in her relations with the patient and held forth the hope of divine forgiveness. After some of the purification ceremonies, the *curandera* complimented Catalina on her devotion.

The treatment ended six months after it began. When Catalina came one day for her appointed flogging, the *curandera* instead asked the patient to join her in prayer. When they rose after the prayer, the *curandera* laid her hands on Catalina's shoulders and solemnly announced that God had forgiven her. With tears of joy in her eyes, the *curandera* embraced her patient and whispered that God loved Catalina for so faithfully repaying the world for her sin. She told her to return to the world and live a normal life. A week later, Catalina's parents gave a party to thank God for his blessing. Society welcomed Catalina home again.

The *curanderos* are not fully aware of the extent to which they cure by social manipulation and psychotherapy. Many *curanderos* are unrecognized but highly skilled social workers. The successful resolution of the social conflict responsible for the illness usually relieves psychosomatic symptoms and reenforces belief in the reality of the folk diseases as well as the *curandero's* ability to cure them.

The danger of folk medicine lies in the possibility of mistaking a contagious or malignant disease for one of the folk diseases, such as *susto* or *empacho.* The high incidence of tuberculosis among the Latin population of the Magic Valley is partly due to the fact that it is commonly misdiagnosed as *susto pasado.* There is no doubt that cases of tuberculosis and cancer have run their fatal course while the patients were being treated with cleansings and prayer. The solution of this problem depends on a two-way process of education among the Anglo and Latin populations.

12

Education, Politics, and Progress

The Language Barrier

MRS. LEWIS IS A DEDICATED TEACHER who has a deep affection for the Mexican-Americans in the Magic Valley. "They are good people," she said. "Their only handicap is the bag full of superstitions and silly notions they inherited from Mexico. When they get rid of these superstitions they will be good Americans. The schools help more than anything else. In time, the Latins will think and act like Americans. A lot depends on whether we can get them to switch from Spanish to English. When they speak Spanish they think Mexican. When the day comes that they speak English at home like the rest of us they will be part of the American way of life." Mrs. Lewis paused with a worried look and added, "I just don't understand why they are so insistent about using Spanish. They should realize that it's not the American tongue."

From the Anglo viewpoint, Spanish is the primary symbol of the "foreignness" of the Mexican-American. For the Latin, Spanish is the primary symbol of loyalty to *La Raza.* The Mexican-American who speaks English in a gathering of conservative Latins is mocked and regarded as a traitor to *La Raza.* Among members of the lower class, such linguistic disloyalty is forgiven only when a man is drunk. "Luis was so drunk last night," said Manuel, "that he was speaking English. He talked nonsense and said things without meaning. He was out of his head but he had a good time."

Because of the exclusive use of Spanish in the home, most children from lower-class families know very little English when they enter school. To remedy this linguistic handicap, the schools conduct a commendable program of preschool instruction in English. The language problem faced by Mexican-American school children is indeed serious. As Mrs. Lewis said, "These children may seem backward at first but it's not their fault. They just don't understand what is being said in class. They are bright but they don't speak our language."

Today a virtual crusade is going on in the Magic Valley to encourage the exclusive use of English. Most schools punish pupils for speaking Spanish on the school grounds. Until recently, no Spanish classes were offered in the elementary schools. As a result, most Mexican-Americans of the lower classes cannot read or write Spanish. The schools make a concerted effort to convince Mexican-American students that they should adopt English as their primary language. Teachers urge them to remember that English is the official language of this country and a mark of good citizenship. One school held a poster-making contest entitled "Why good citizens speak English." The majority of the posters elaborated on patriotic themes such as "'Americans speak English" and "Texans Speak English." Some of the poster artists saw other advantages. One junior-high student drew two pictures showing herself before and after she had mastered English. The first one showed her alone with a puzzled expression on her face. The second picture showed her surrounded by boys. The caption read, "If You Want Dates, Speak English!"

Teachers regularly visit the homes of their Mexican-American students to encourage the parents to use English at home. Such visits are seldom welcomed because the average teacher unwittingly violates every rule of Latin etiquette, leaving behind a feeling of hostility. Juan recalled a visit from his youngest child's teacher:

> She burst in here like a rooster without even waiting for an invitation. Then, she started telling me what to do. This is my home and I will decide what is done here. And she tried to tell me not to speak the language of my forefathers. She does not understand nor does she want to. My children go to school to learn but they are merely taught not to respect their parents. It is an evil thing. I no longer blame my children for not liking the school.

For the Latin child from a lower-class family, school is often a bewildering and hostile environment. He hears the teaching of his parents contradicted and he is urged to behave in ways that are uncomfortable for him. Mexican-American children especially dread being forced to recite in class. They know that their mistakes in English will be criticized in class and perhaps ridiculed after class by Anglo students. The push to excel and compete for grades violates the noncompetitive values of *La Raza.* A Mexican-American student who conspicuously outshines his age-mates in academic endeavors is mocked or shunned. Children of crop pickers face even greater difficulties and may fall hopelessly behind in their school work during long absences when they join their families on the annual migration at harvesting time.

Differences in outlook and behavior tend to socially segregate the Mexican-Americans from the Anglo students although they attend integrated classes. During recess or social gatherings, the usual pattern is for Mexican-American students to stick together apart from the Anglos. Even the informality of the high-school dance rarely breaks through this apartness. A Latin youth may dance with an Anglo girl but when the music stops, he returns to the other Mexican-Americans and she rejoins the Anglo students. Integrated dancing is a recent phenomenon and the social discomfort of the dancers is often apparent. An Anglo chaperon at a school dance commented, "Those poor Mexican kids don't seem to know what they are supposed to do. They can't relax except when they are with their own kind. When a Mexican is with Anglos, he either plays the part of a stuffed shirt or a fool. I wonder whether the Mexicans themselves know what they want."

Lack of Goal Orientation

A good many of the Mexican-Americans who go on to college don't seem to know what they want out of an education. This lack of purpose is particularly characteristic of Latins who are seeking a higher education than their parents received. Mexican-Americans from upper-class families usually have a specific goal in mind. They study to become doctors or lawyers or to acquire the well-rounded education of a gentleman. In contrast, Latins from the lower and middle classes who go to college rarely come out qualified for a profession or well-paid occupation.

Pete is the son of middle-class parents who financed his four years at the University of Texas. While he was there, he changed his major several times and graduated as a "C" student in history. Today he is a clerk in his father's small store. Sometimes, he talks about going back to school to study engineering. He is not sure that he would like to be an engineer, however, and he thinks a Latin engineer might have trouble getting a job in the Magic Valley. He knows that his father wants him to take over the store some day. "My parents are sure proud of my degree," Pete said, "but I didn't learn a darn thing in college that is going to help me be a better store keeper. I guess I'll keep the old man happy and stay on with him. I'll let my kids be the engineers."

The characteristic lack of goal orientation among high-school and college students from lower- and middle-class families often distresses their elders. One Mexican-American educator blames this shortcoming of the younger generation on the scarcity of job opportunities for educated Latins:

> Unless the qualified Latin gets out of the valley, he doesn't have much chance. When a firm has its choice of a Latin or an Anglo with equal ability, the Anglo gets the job every time unless the firm is having financial difficulties. Then, the employers hire the Latin at an unfair salary and talk about how broadminded they are. I tell my young Latin friends who have ability or training to get out and go to Chicago or Los Angeles. But, being Latin, they don't want to leave their families so they stay here and grow bitter.

A Mexican-American mother from a conservative, middle-class home is worried about her two sons. One is attending high school and the other is in college. "These kids!" she sighed. "They are like lost souls. They wander around looking for excitement. They don't seem to enjoy themselves unless they are drinking or chasing girls. I just hope they don't get into trouble. I don't know why they waste their time looking for thrills when they should be studying."

Her sons do not know how to cope with the conflict between the Anglo values they learn in school and the Latin values learned at home. As one son put it, "I don't know whether I am a Mexican or an American. I guess I'm neither."

Mexican-Americans caught in the middle of the conflict between two cultures may react in one of several ways. Some retreat to the security of the conservative Mexican-American world. Some seek geographical escape by migrating to the larger cities of Texas or to California, Michigan, or Illinois. Some escape into the twilight zone of alcoholism. Some rebel and commit crimes or engage in antisocial behavior. As their numbers increase, more and more acculturated Mexican-Americans are trying to create for themselves a respected place embracing the best of both worlds.

Middle-Class Political Movements

John Salazar is a representative member of the middle-class group that seeks the advantages of acculturation but opposes assimilation with the Anglo majority. He explained his position:

> My first name is English and my second name is Spanish. My ancestry is Mexican but if you ask me what I am, I'll tell you I'm an American and I'm a good American. I've worked for this country and fought for it. I would also die for it. But I want the right to be my own kind of American. I would no more renounce my Mexican heritage than the Anglos would renounce the English language. I am just as American as the Anglos but my ancestors came from Mexico. I'm a Mexican-American and I'm proud of it. We Mexican-Americans can contribute to the greatness of our country. All we need to do is organize, state our wishes, and vote.

Men like John Salazar are beginning to succeed in making themselves felt. They are the backbone of the Latin American political movements that are daily gathering strength and followers. In the early part of the twentieth century, members of the Latin lower class voted only under the direction of an Anglo political boss who did them favors. When such practices were ended by the forces of good government, the lower-class Latins seldom took the trouble to vote. They assumed that all politicians were crooked so it didn't much matter which one got elected. None of the candidates promised to help the Mexican-Americans until very recent times. Today, things are different. A constantly growing part of the Latin population is learning the value of group political action from observing Negro victories and those of Latin organizations such as Political Action for Spanish Speaking Organizations.

Enrique is a member of the lower class who voted for the first time when he was fifty years old. He explained why, "We have three choices. We can keep on picking cotton for peanuts. We can become gringos. Or, if we are men enough, we can gather our strength, conquer our weaknesses, and stand together to run this part of the state. We have knelt in the dust too long. We have learned to play baseball as a team. We can also learn to play politics as a team. We are good baseball players."

John Salazar wants to speed up the growth of Latin political power. He thinks a positive program backed by the right leaders would help. "Most Latins don't know how to think politically," he said. "We complain and complain about what is wrong but very few of us speak up and state exactly what we want. We need to shout our demands instead of whining about our grievances."

When asked what he wanted for the Mexican-Americans, John answered:

> We want equal opportunities for jobs and equal pay for equal work. We want to share the material benefits of American technology. We also want the right to be different from the Anglos. We want to maintain the Mexican family, the dignity of the individual, and the beauty of the Spanish language. I would never trade Latin dignity for Anglo boistrousness. I don't want to be like my Anglo neighbors. I want to be John Salazar, a Mexican-American. This country should be big enough to allow us the freedom to be different without being oppressed.

The John Salazars of Texas are the leaders of such organizations as League of United Latin American Citizens, PASO, and the Catholic War Veterans. They foresee a rapid expansion in the political strength of these groups and hope they will all join forces in time. "Then, we will be heard," said John. "Then ethnic rights will be more important than state's rights."

Bob Campos disapproves of Salazar's ideas. Campos has made it into the Anglo world. He is a successful doctor, a civic leader, and a highly respected man in the Anglo community. He drives a Buick, votes Democratic, and serves on a committee that is working to end Negro segregation. He is highly skilled in his profession but takes little interest in literature or the arts. His favorite leisure activities are golf and a game of poker at his lodge. When asked about Mexican-American problems, he bristled. "How should I know about them?" he countered. "I don't even speak their language." On another occasion, however, he expressed the hope that his children would learn Spanish in college. "We live in an international age," Dr. Campos said. "I think every American should learn at least one foreign language."

Epilogue

by Andre Guerrero

MEXICAN-AMERICAN RESENTMENT of Anglo domination in South Texas has been smoldering a long time, but it did not result in organized confrontations until the advent of the Chicano movement during the late sixties. Beginning with a farm workers' strike in the Lower Rio Grande Valley, the movement was joined by young Chicanos who organized a series of demonstrations protesting unfair treatment by Anglo police, judges, and school administrators.

In some cases, entire families participated in student protests to show support for their children. Despite such striking evidence of family solidarity, the Chicano movement has not received unanimous support among the Mexican-Americans of South Texas. There are some who agree with the goals but not the tactics of confrontations which frequently end in violence.

In this epilogue, Andre Guerrero discusses Chicanismo from a Chicano point of view. Not all Mexican-Americans will agree with his views (or mine) but he has made a significant contribution to our understanding of Chicano aims and attitudes. Guerrero was born and raised in Laredo, Texas. He received his B.A. at St. Edward's University in Austin and his M.A. in education at Antioch College. After teaching school in Detroit, he joined the staff of the Southwest Educational Development Laboratory in Austin. He later served as Acting Director of Curriculum at the National Center for Bilingual and Bicultural Education in Forth Worth, Texas. Currently, he is co-director of the Juarez-Lincoln Center in Austin.

William Madsen

"Por Mi Raza Hablará El Espíritu"

I am Joaquin
lost in a world of confusion,
caught up in a whirl of a
gringo society,
confused by the rules,
scorned by attitudes,
suppressed by manipulations,
and destroyed by modern society.
My fathers
have lost the economic battle
and won
the struggle of cultural survival.
And now!
I must choose
between
the paradox of
victory of the spirit,
despite physical hunger
or
to exist in the grasp
of American social neurosis,
sterilization of the soul . . .
from *Yo Soy Joaquin*
by Rodolfo Gonzales

We are thankful that no great unpleasantness has taken place in Texas as an outgrowth of the efforts to bring about a recognition of the rights of citizenship of those belonging to minority groups. We submit that the exercise of force of undue pressure from any quarter to accomplish any objective can only serve to engender bitterness and resentment which inevitably will delay the realization of just and righteous aims. . . .
from *The 50 States Report* submitted to the Commission on Civil Rights by the State Advisory Committees, 1961.

The Mexican-American of the lower Rio Grande Valley is special. His roots, geographical and cultural, are but a few miles away. He confronts them constantly. How he reacts to these roots makes him a Latin American, a Mexican-American, or a Chicano. All are a part of *La Raza* and all are affected by those who neither understand nor desire that *La Raza* should assume its place as the dominant political and economic force in South Texas.

The valley is *La Cuna*[1] of Chicanismo in Texas. From here the land

[1] The cradle.

and its culture send out the vital force that is the migrant stream reaching the major agricultural centers of the country. *Los migrantes*[2] take with them their families, their language, and their labor, infusing the spirit of *La Raza* with Chicanismo as they make contact with other Chicanos. Those who stay behind in the valley—the nonmigrant poor, the middle-class Chicanos, and the wealthy—are engaged in their own dialogue with their culture and that of the Anglo.

In most cities of the valley, Anglos control the city councils. Anglos control the police stations. Anglos control the banks, the school boards, and the schools. And Anglos control the news media. But the valley is Chicano. The *ambiente*[3] is Chicano. The vitality, the complexion, and the change forces are all Chicano.

Things are changing in the valley today. *La Raza* has begun to effect its own resolution of the paradox that confronts its Brown sons. The "unpleasantness" and "undue pressure" so feared in the Civil Rights Commission Report of a decade ago have now become realities. Police brutality, White apathy, and Anglo incomprehension have forced *La Raza's* hand. How we have responded and continue to respond will be our own definition of who we are and what we, as *La Raza*, must be. In our own land and among our own people we are claiming, at last, the right to shape our own identity.

Just how much longer Chicano "containment" by the Anglo will last is debatable. That a take-over is coming is sensed by Anglos and declared by Chicanos in confrontations asserting the right of self-determination. The reaction to these confrontations has been a surfacing resentment among Whites who say "things are better now than they ever have been for Mexican-Americans." How much better living conditions are now than they were in the 1930s is a matter of opinion. Recently I compared notes on migrant housing, sewage, and medical attention with Russell Lee, a member of the Farm Securities Team that photographed migrant conditions in the valley during the depression. It seemed that we were both talking about identical living conditions. The migrant communities had not changed in 40 years. Water was still being hauled in by the barrel and sewage facilities were nonexistent. I visited migrant homes this spring where the streets were unpaved, the dust, heat, and humidity unbearable.

The Chicano movement in Texas began in 1966 with a farm workers' strike. It was the first of many subsequent confrontations. Workers at La Casita Farms in Starr County chose the crucial picking time of the cantaloupe crop to voice their demands for free, democratic elections leading to unionization. The valuable cantaloupe crop ruins quickly if not picked in time. This was the time to strike. With Cesar Chavez' example[4] as an impetus, the workers at La Casita Farms began their boycott of the California-based firm.

Antonio Orendain, Reynaldo de la Cruz, Juan Dimas, and Bill Chandler became leaders of the effort. When La Casita began bringing in Mexican

---

[2] The migrants.

[3] Atmosphere.

[4] Cesar Chavez led the farm workers' strike at Delano, California.

nationals from across the border, Orendain and the strikers went to the international bridge and distributed leaflets explaining to the Mexicans the reasons why they were being urged to join the boycott. When United States officials attempted to arrest the group, they stepped across the boundary line to the Mexican side of the border. When Mexican officials attempted to detain them, they walked the short distance back to the United States side of the border. When this maneuver proved unsuccessful, the group lay down on the bridge and the Texas Rangers were called in. Subsequent harassment further embittered *La Raza* against the Rangers, and one lawsuit is still pending against them as a result of their role in the strike.

Violence erupted several times. A bridge was burned to stop the shipment of the cantaloupes. Brutality was charged as the strikers and sympathetic activists began their march to Austin, Texas, over 300 miles away to take their case to the state capitol. State officials refused to meet with the strikers. Months later, after the depletion of food and medical supplies and a $5.00 a week allowance per family, the workers began the exodus which led them to jobs in the North.

La Casita did not give in but the strike was not in vain. Valuable lessons in organizing were learned. The positions taken on the strike by Mexican-Americans and Anglos identified those who could be counted on to take risks for *La Raza.* The spirit of the strike gave strong power to the Chicano movement in the valley. Political lessons learned during the strike were significant. *La Raza* would never forget how the Democrats responded to the strikers when they reached Austin. The political suasion which the Democrats traditionally held with Mexican-Americans was broken. The rift began at Pan American University in Edinburg, Texas, where the Young Democrats formed a group called "Mexicanos Para Tower" to support John Tower, the Republican candidate for the United States Senate. Tower's subsequent victory over his Democratic opponent was attributed in part to the support he received from Mexican-Americans.

A turning point in Hidalgo County politics was the election held in November of 1970. In the first "upset" in decades, a Mexican-American named Ed Gomez unseated the county judge and began the movement to make political control of the valley more representative of its population. The Anglo judge unseated by Gomez had alienated Mexican-Americans by holding a Chicano leader in contempt of court because he refused to state his name. When Jesus Ramirez appeared in court as a spokesman for reform he refused to give his name saying it was unimportant. What counted, he said, was his mission before the judge. A vigil was held outside the court to protest the judge's action.

The Hidalgo County election also served as a testing ground for a third party known as Raza Unida. Alejandro Moreno ran on the Raza Unida ticket as a candidate for County Commissioner. Although he lost the election, Moreno received a majority of the votes cast in San Juan, Texas, and a near majority in Alamo, Texas. The strength of his support gave Chicanos hope that the Raza Unida party could offer a much-needed springboard for Chicano candidates. In April 1971, the people of San Juan, Texas, elected a Mexican-American mayor and two other Mexican-Americans were elected as city commissioners.

The most violent confrontation took place in Pharr, Texas, in February of 1971. Pharr is typical of the small Texas towns where Anglos control wages and politics affecting Chicanos who constitute an unrepresented majority. The agricultural, ranching, oil, and commercial czars who rule these communities control the jobs, the schools, the courts, and the federal funds. The only Mexican-Americans who can challenge Anglo control and survive economically are those who are independently wealthy. Chicanos who are part of the city power structure usually serve as petty functionaries or law enforcement henchmen for their Anglo bosses. Such conditions breed the resentment that was manifested in Pharr on February 7, 1971.

Police brutality was the issue that Saturday when a small group of Mexican-Americans displayed signs calling for an end to police harassment. By nightfall a 20-year-old Mexican-American was dead. His hands were still in his pockets when the ambulance came. Poncho Loredo Flores had been standing on a corner watching the protest when he was shot. Several witnesses claimed he was shot by a policeman. Flores was unarmed, as were the other Mexican-Americans, when police riot troops and the Texas Rangers were called in to put an end to the unlawful assembly. The mayor had not issued a parade permit to anyone for that day. Unarmed men, teenagers, and women were gassed and firehosed until they threw rocks in self-defense. Then the officers fired on the marchers. A Civil Rights investigation resulted in no indictments.

A sense of outrage swept over Mexican-American communities throughout the valley reaching even middle-class conservatives who were not militants. They found what appeared to them to be indiscriminate gassing, arrests, and bludgeonings too much to tolerate. I talked with several teachers who supported reports that innocent bystanders were subjected to police brutality simply because they happened to be in the downtown area of Pharr at the time of the protest. The victims included those who were spending a Saturday afternoon in restaurants, cafes, and recreation centers.

The Pharr riot awakened Mexican-Americans who had not been involved in the protest movement. They saw how Chicanos were met with swift, brutal repression for presenting an issue that challenged the conduct of law enforcement agents. The jolt issued by the bullets and sirens on the streets of Pharr reverberated in other towns where police brutality had also occurred. The killing, whether by the police or someone else, of an apparently innocent Chicano was not something that could be easily dismissed or forgotten in the valley for here protest marches had produced few casualties.

The riot, the election, and the strike reveal only the spring shoots and not the germinating roots of the Chicano movement. Less dramatic but more significant evidence for the growing spiritual strength of Chicanos is to be found elsewhere. It is the quiet, strong "*ya Basta*"[5] of a father whose son is discriminated against in school or a man's decision to speak out against his employer at a great risk that affirms our *machismo*.[6] The quality of spirit witnessed

---

[5] Enough!

[6] Manliness.

here is overwhelming. There is day-to-day involvement of entire families with the struggle to maintain their culture, their education, and their goodwill in the face of inhumane treatment.

As with other peoples and other assaults on the human spirit, our struggle has solidified and vitalized those core values that Mexican-Americans hold dear: the family solidarity, the *carnalismo*,[7] and the affirmation of the worth of the unique, individual self. I find evidence for the strength of these values in the way *Raza* speaks out, organizes, and endures in the face of threats to its freedom both within and without the Mexican-American community.

The testimony before the United States Commission on Civil Rights held in San Antonio, Texas, in 1968 gave the country a realistic report on the Chicano's life in the Southwest. What most Chicanos feel and want for their brothers is well defined in the words of those from the valley who testified at the hearing. Mr. and Mrs. Jose M. Martinez and their 16-year-old son, a migrant family from the valley, spoke on December 12 of their lives as farm laborers. Mother, father, and son work together six months of the year in irregular farm work, picking peppers and tomatoes and hoeing cotton. They are paid an average of $5.00 a day.

Here is the dialogue between the commissioner and Mr. Martinez:

> *Commissioner Garcia.*[8] Mr. Martinez, you naturally are a father, and you are a resident of Texas. Let's say—we would say that you are interested in that Mexican-American people would be organizing a farm union, and they would have better salaries in order to obtain the things that you as a father and as a resident of our State know that the other people have—the good things, good homes, good food, good education for your children. Could you tell us if this is the only reason or the main reason why you work and you fight for your rights and you want that the working people be organized?
>
> *Mr. Martinez.* In the first place that the salaries would be well paying. So they can send the children to school and can buy the books because the books are sold in school. We don't have enough to buy books and give them their proper schooling. Many times you want to study mechanics and you have to pay—and there is not enough, and there would be something better for a citizen of United States to pay a salary of $1.35 or $1.40 for work or even $1.25. And then we could live well and eat well and dress well and we could be proper because sometimes we are ashamed, we are ashamed to go someplace, a place like this because that is why many people don't come here to audience like this. If we don't make enough money, if we don't make the salary that is promised us, then we cannot educate our children properly, and they are always going to be outside of school because we don't have enough to pay for this.
>
> We have to work together in order to earn a minimum salary. Almost the majority of the people in the Valley have a need, many of them. Many of them want that streets would be fixed so that the school bus can come

[7] Brotherhood.

[8] Hector P. Garcia, M.D., member, United States Commission on Civil Rights.

to pick up their children—they have to walk sometimes about a mile when it is cold, when it is raining, there is mud and they get their clothes dirty and the bus only reaches the main highway and they have to walk to the main highway.

And the county doesn't pay any attention to us because it says that the people that sold us there should have put gravel so that the bus can go—or a pipe for drainage so that the bus can get in and we don't have that.

There are colonias in which life is very sad and very hard. It is very muddy and in order to go to a doctor you can't even use a car, you have to take a stretcher to take the persons out of the place. This is in Colonia Hidalgo and Las Milpas and all those places.

If the Government would make the effort to take care of the needs of the people, of the American people, or the citizens of this country, they could do it. What they could do, the people would live—would be much happier, people would talk to one another. That is all I have to say.[9]

In 1967 a self-help organization known as Colonias del Valle was created following the destruction of Hurricane Beulah to aid families living in the 180 colonias of the valley. The colonia is a group of several hundred families, Mexican-American, who live on the outskirts of the larger cities in the valley. Most families are farm workers. Colonias del Valle is representative of the growing political and organizational activism of the Chicano. Trinidad Piña, a Chicano student at Colegio Jacinto Treviño, now heads Colonias del Valle which works with over 23 local organizations from individual colonias on survival issues such as water, sewage, and food. Most colonias have no water or sewage facilities and they need surplus food commodity aid. Trini Piña carries the responsibility for the economic survival of a great number of his people.

Family participation in the Chicano movement has been an important factor in its growth. Entire families marched together in the farm workers' strike. Grandfathers, uncles, and teenagers picketed in Pharr. The work of Colonias del Valle received the support of many migrant families. When one considers the strong bond linking generations of Chicanos who have suffered the same injustices, he can begin to understand how this powerful common experience welds together the nuclear and extended family. Several generations living in the same house share a sense of continuity reaching back for decades.

Perhaps it is in the context of the student protest movement that the nature of family solidarity can best be described. There is no dichotomy between generations in activist families. When the young Chicano decides he has had enough, that the prejudice and discrimination has to stop, often his action is supported by the whole family including several generations. The student demands for equal representation on student councils, cheerleader squads, and honor societies in predominantly Mexican-American schools and for Mexican-American counsellors, teachers, and administrators are but the youthful expres-

---

[9] Hearing before the United States Commission on Civil Rights, hearing held in San Antonio, Texas, December 9–14, 1968. United States Government Printing Office; 1969–0–358–411, pp. 441–442.

sion of that need for justice and respect his parents and grandparents fight for in their own spheres of action. I know of entire families who went into action to support a boycotting son or daughter. In one case the father worked at the same school where his son led a walkout. He lost his job as a result of his support for his son.

The first noteworthy student protest in the valley was a walkout in Edcouch-Elsa organized in 1968 by Javier Ramirez, leader of the Mexican-American Youth Organization known as M.A.Y.O. Their unmet demands included: abolishment of punishment for speaking Spanish on the school grounds, more teachers who understood Chicanos, and curriculum relevant to Chicano history and culture. When several hundred students boycotted the schools, a Chicano superintendent from a neighboring school district offered classes in his schools to the students. Parents of most students, including the walkout leaders, supported the boycott. Similar student protests occurred in Weslaco and McAllen in 1969. The following year McAllen students organized another protest when the first Mexican-American president of the student council was removed from office reportedly because of his affiliation with M.A.Y.O., which is considered by many to be a radical organization.

By far the most ambitious educational project undertaken by Chicanos in the Southwest emerged from a M.A.Y.O. conference held in December, 1969, at La Lomita chapel near Mission, Texas. Here the idea of establishing a Chicano college was first proposed. The purpose of the college would be to train teachers capable of meeting the special needs of Chicano children. Their needs have long been neglected by the schools. Bilingual programs, bicultural curriculum, and trained Chicano teachers are affecting but a fraction of the Mexican-American enrollment in valley schools.

What happened during the next ten months brought together an impressive group of Chicano students, artists, educators, migrants, and politicians. To start a college from scratch, they drew up plans for curriculum, funding, students, faculty, materials, physical plant, and accreditation. The dominant spirit behind the colegio was brilliant, articulate Aurelio Montemayor who gathered together a cadre of 15 Chicanos. Narciso Aleman of the Colorado Migrant Council began laying the groundwork for funding and accreditation.

The nation's first Chicano college, a graduate school, was dedicated on October 11, 1970. It was named after Jacinto Treviño, a valley folk hero who had successfully routed the Texas Rangers in decades past. Colegio Jacinto Treviño began the organized attempt to build parallel institutions in the Southwest which would be responsive to the needs of Chicanos.

A series of position papers providing the intellectual impetus for the colegio read like a blueprint for educational change in the Southwest. Problems of bilingualism and biculturalism were defined and explored by Marta Cotera, one of the nation's most respected Chicano leaders. Juan Cotera, poet, architect, city planner, and philosopher, outlined the institution's responsibility to the community. Juan Rivera wrote on the linguistic problems of Chicano children with whom the colegio would be working. Aurelio Montemayor wrote on the selection of Chicanos for faculty and staff.

Dean of the colegio was Dr. Leonard Mestas, the dynamic force behind reform in Colorado's programs for migrant children. When Dr. Mestas went to Washington, D.C., to try to get funding for the colegio he was informed that he had become known as the dean of a college operating "off the back of a truck." He lived in his red van for several weeks after the colegio opened.

Colegio Jacinto Treviño received its accreditation from the Antioch Graduate School of Education. The first Anglos to sponsor a graduate school designed and run entirely by Chicanos were: James Dixon, president of Antioch College; Morris Keeton, academic vice-president; and Robert Piper, dean of Antioch Graduate School.

The students of the colegio were activist leaders from South Texas and California. Several came from migrant families and had worked as migrants themselves. During the first few weeks of school the colegio met in student homes. There was no building. The colegio consisted of 15 students and the faculty, an impressive group of educators who donated their time off from other teaching duties.

In January 1971 the college settled into its first home in Mercedes, Texas. There the controversial undertaking has provoked internal and external debate which still continues. But it was a start. It proved that Chicanos could take responsibility for their own education. And it was born in the valley—*La Cuna* of Chicanismo in Texas.

The valley is different when the migrants leave. Their homes boarded up and still, the colonias quiet, all seem to be waiting for their return. The schools begin emptying early in spring as the migrant children start the trip to follow the crops with their parents.

I sense that all Chicanos, those who migrate and those who stay behind, go with the migrants. They are *La Raza*'s most treasured resource for they experience so intensely the problems we all bear. And they survive. *La Raza* embraces all Chicanos, all Mexican-Americans, and all Latin Americans, as do the arms of the migrant stream. We have a common spirit which alone makes all of us *Raza.* And it is enough. For the Southwest sun and the Southwest earth will keep us Brown and *La Raza* with Brown love and Brown orgasm will endure.

Recommended Reading

CLARK, MARGARET, *Health in the Mexican-American Culture: A Community Study*. Berkeley: University of California Press, 1959.

An ethnographic study of a Latin group in San Jose, California.

EDMUNDSON, MUNRO, *Los Manitos*. New Orleans: Middle American Research Institute, Tulane University, 1957.

A study of the values of the Spanish-speaking people in New Mexico.

HUDSON, WILSON M. (Ed.), *The Healer of Los Olmos*. Dallas: 1951.

The story of Don Pedro Jaramillo, the most famous *curandero* of the borderland.

KIBBE, PAULINE, *Latin Americans in Texas*. Albuquerque: The University of New Mexico Press, 1946.

A generalized survey of the social and economic problems of the Latin population.

MADSEN, WILLIAM, *Society and Health in the Lower Rio Grande Valley*. Austin: Hogg Foundation for Mental Health, The University of Texas, 1961.

An analysis of conflicting cultural attitudes toward disease with recommendations for implementing public-health programs in Hidalgo County. Texas.

MCWILLIAMS, CAREY, *North From Mexico: The Spanish-Speaking People of the United States*. Philadelphia: J. B. Lippincott Company, 1948.

An exposé of injustices suffered by Mexican-Americans.

PAREDES, AMÉRICO, *With His Pistol in His Hand*. Austin: University of Texas Press, 1958.

The well-told tale of a border ballad and its Mexican-American hero.

ROMANO, OCTAVIO, Donship in a Mexican-American community in Texas. *American Anthropologist*, 62, 966–976, 1960.

A perceptive analysis of the prestige system in a frontier folk society.

RUBEL, ARTHUR J., Concepts of Disease in Mexican-American Culture. *American Anthropologist,* 62:795–814, 1960.

Explains the reinforcement of belief in several folk diseases and cures.

SÁNCHEZ, GEORGE, *Forgotten People.* Albuquerque: University of New Mexico Press, 1940.

A study of the Indian, Spanish, and Anglo groups in New Mexico written by a distinguished educator.

SAUNDERS, LYLE, *Cultural Differences and Medical Care: The Case of the Spanish-Speaking People of the Southwest.* New York: Russell Sage Foundation, 1954.

A discussion of the different social relationships and cultural expectations involved in the medical systems of Anglo and Latin groups.

STAMBAUGH, J. LEE AND LILLIAN J., *The Lower Rio Grande Valley of Texas.* San Antonio, Tex.: The Naylor Co., 1954.

A history of the Texas borderland.